Lecture Notes in Computer Science 12993

Bedir Tekinerdogan · Yingwei Wang ·
Liang-Jie Zhang (Eds.)

Internet of Things – ICIOT 2021

6th International Conference
Held as Part of the Services Conference Federation, SCF 2021
Virtual Event, December 10–14, 2021
Proceedings

Springer

Editors
Bedir Tekinerdogan
Wageningen University Maatschappijw
Wageningen, The Netherlands

Yingwei Wang
University of Prince Edward Island
Charlottetown, Canada

Liang-Jie Zhang (ID)
Kingdee International Software Group
Co., Ltd.
Shenzhen, China

ISSN 0302-9743   ISSN 1611-3349 (electronic)
Lecture Notes in Computer Science
ISBN 978-3-030-96067-4   ISBN 978-3-030-96068-1 (eBook)
https://doi.org/10.1007/978-3-030-96068-1

LNCS Sublibrary: SL1 – Theoretical Computer Science and General Issues

This Springer imprint is published by the registered company Springer Nature Switzerland AG
The registered company address is: Gewerbestrasse 11, 6330 Cham, Switzerland

Preface

With the rapid advancements of mobile Internet, cloud computing, and big data, the traditional device-centric Internet of Things (IoT) is now moving into a new era which is termed Internet of Things Services (IoTS). In this era, sensors and other types of sensing devices; wired and wireless networks; platforms and tools; data processing, visualization, analysis, and integration engines; and other components of traditional IoT are interconnected through innovative services to realize the value of connected things, people, and virtual Internet spaces. The way of building new IoT applications is changing. We indeed need creative thinking, long-term visions, and innovative methodologies to respond to such a change. The ICIOT 2021 conference was organized to promote research and application innovations around the world.

ICIOT is a member of Services Conference Federation (SCF). SCF 2021 featured the following 10 collocated service-oriented sister conferences: the International Conference on Web Services (ICWS 2021), the International Conference on Cloud Computing (CLOUD 2021), the International Conference on Services Computing (SCC 2021), the International Conference on Big Data (BigData 2021), the International Conference on AI and Mobile Services (AIMS 2021), the World Congress on Services (SERVICES 2021), the International Conference on Internet of Things (ICIOT 2021), the International Conference on Cognitive Computing (ICCC 2021), the International Conference on Edge Computing (EDGE 2021), and the International Conference on Blockchain (ICBC 2021).

This volume presents the accepted papers for ICIOT 2021, held virtually over the Internet during December 10–14, 2021. For ICIOT 2021, we accepted eight papers for the proceedings. Each paper was reviewed by at least three independent members of the ICIOT 2021 Program Committee.

We are pleased to thank the authors whose submissions and participation made this conference possible. We also want to express our thanks to the Organizing Committee and Program Committee members for their dedication in helping to organize the conference and reviewing the submissions. We look forward to your future contributions as volunteers, authors, and conference participants in the fast-growing worldwide services innovations community.

December 2021

Bedir Tekinerdogan
Yingwei Wang
Liang-Jie Zhang

Organization

ICIOT 2021 General Chair

Min Luo   Georgia Tech, USA

ICIOT 2021 Program Chairs

Bedir Tekinerdogan   Wageningen University, The Netherlands
Yingwei Wang   University of Prince Edward Island, Canada

Services Conference Federation (SCF 2021)

General Chairs

Wu Chou   Essenlix Corporation, USA
Calton Pu (Co-chair)   Georgia Tech, USA
Dimitrios Georgakopoulos   Swinburne University of Technology, Australia

Program Chairs

Liang-Jie Zhang   Kingdee International Software Group Co., Ltd.,
                                     China
Ali Arsanjani   Amazon Web Services, USA

CFO

Min Luo   Georgia Tech, USA

Industry Track Chairs

Awel Dico   Etihad Airways, UAE
Rajesh Subramanyan   Amazon Web Services, USA
Siva Kantamneni   Deloitte Consulting, UK

Industry Exhibit and International Affairs Chair

Zhixiong Chen   Mercy College, USA

Operations Committee

Jing Zeng   China Gridcom Co., Ltd., China
Yishuang Ning   Tsinghua University, China
Sheng He   Tsinghua University, China

Steering Committee

Calton Pu (Co-chair)   Georgia Tech, USA
Liang-Jie Zhang (Co-chair)   Kingdee International Software Group Co., Ltd.,
                                     China

ICIOT 2021 Program Committee

Abdurazzag Aburas   University of Kwazulu Natal, South Africa
Georgios Bouloukakis   Telecom SudParis, France
Luca Cagliero   Politecnico di Torino, Italy
Tao Chen   University of Birmingham, UK
Marisol García-Valls   Universitat Politecnica de Valencia, Spain
Franck Le   IBM T. J. Watson Research Center, USA
Yutao Ma   Wuhan University, China
Rui André Oliveira   University of Lisbon, Portugal
Françoise Sailhan   CNAM, France
Jian Wang   Wuhan University, China
Na Yu   Samsung Research America, USA
Liang-Jie Zhang   Kingdee International Software Group Co., Ltd.,
                                     China

Conference Sponsor – Services Society

The Services Society (S2) is a non-profit professional organization that has been created to promote worldwide research and technical collaboration in services innovations among academia and industrial professionals. Its members are volunteers from industry and academia with common interests. S2 is registered in the USA as a "501(c) organization", which means that it is an American tax-exempt nonprofit organization. S2 collaborates with other professional organizations to sponsor or co-sponsor conferences and to promote an effective services curriculum in colleges and universities. S2 initiates and promotes a "Services University" program worldwide to bridge the gap between industrial needs and university instruction.

The services sector accounted for 79.5% of the GDP of the USA in 2016. Hong Kong has one of the world's most service-oriented economies, with the services sector accounting for more than 90% of GDP. As such, the Services Society has formed 10 Special Interest Groups (SIGs) to support technology and domain specific professional activities:

- Special Interest Group on Web Services (SIG-WS)
- Special Interest Group on Services Computing (SIG-SC)
- Special Interest Group on Services Industry (SIG-SI)
- Special Interest Group on Big Data (SIG-BD)
- Special Interest Group on Cloud Computing (SIG-CLOUD)
- Special Interest Group on Artificial Intelligence (SIG-AI)
- Special Interest Group on Edge Computing (SIG-EC)
- Special Interest Group on Cognitive Computing (SIG-CC)
- Special Interest Group on Blockchain (SIG-BC)
- Special Interest Group on Internet of Things (SIG-IOT)

About the Services Conference Federation (SCF)

As the founding member of the Services Conference Federation (SCF), the First International Conference on Web Services (ICWS) was held in June 2003 in Las Vegas, USA. A sister event, the First International Conference on Web Services - Europe 2003 (ICWS-Europe 2003) was held in Germany in October of the same year. In 2004, ICWS-Europe was changed to the European Conference on Web Services (ECOWS), which was held in Erfurt, Germany. The 19th edition in the conference series, SCF 2021, was held virtually over the Internet during December 10–14, 2021.

In the past 18 years, the ICWS community has expanded from Web engineering innovations to scientific research for the whole services industry. The service delivery platforms have expanded to mobile platforms, the Internet of Things (IoT), cloud computing, and edge computing. The services ecosystem has gradually been enabled, value added, and intelligence embedded through enabling technologies such as big data, artificial intelligence, and cognitive computing. In the coming years, transactions with multiple parties involved will be transformed by blockchain.

Based on the technology trends and best practices in the field, SCF will continue serving as the conference umbrella's code name for all services-related conferences. SCF 2021 defined the future of the New ABCDE (AI, Blockchain, Cloud, big Data, Everything is connected), which enable IoT and support the "5G for Services Era". SCF 2021 featured 10 collocated conferences all centered around the topic of "services", each focusing on exploring different themes (e.g. web-based services, cloud-based services, big data-based services, services innovation lifecycle, AI-driven ubiquitous services, blockchain-driven trust service-ecosystems, industry-specific services and applications, and emerging service-oriented technologies). The SCF 2021 members were as follows:

1. The 2021 International Conference on Web Services (ICWS 2021, http://icws.org/), which was the flagship conference for web-based services featuring web services modeling, development, publishing, discovery, composition, testing, adaptation, and delivery, as well as the latest API standards.
2. The 2021 International Conference on Cloud Computing (CLOUD 2021, http://the cloudcomputing.org/), which was the flagship conference for modeling, developing, publishing, monitoring, managing, and delivering XaaS (everything as a service) in the context of various types of cloud environments.
3. The 2021 International Conference on Big Data (BigData 2021, http://bigdataco ngress.org/), which focused on the scientific and engineering innovations of big data.
4. The 2021 International Conference on Services Computing (SCC 2021, http://the scc.org/), which was the flagship conference for the services innovation lifecycle including enterprise modeling, business consulting, solution creation, services orchestration, services optimization, services management, services marketing, and business process integration and management.

5. The 2021 International Conference on AI and Mobile Services (AIMS 2021, http:// ai1000.org/), which addressed the science and technology of artificial intelligence and the development, publication, discovery, orchestration, invocation, testing, delivery, and certification of AI-enabled services and mobile applications.
6. The 2021 World Congress on Services (SERVICES 2021, http://servicescongress. org/), which put its focus on emerging service-oriented technologies and industry-specific services and solutions.
7. The 2021 International Conference on Cognitive Computing (ICCC 2021, http:// thecognitivecomputing.org/), which put its focus on Sensing Intelligence (SI) as a Service (SIaaS), making a system listen, speak, see, smell, taste, understand, interact, and/or walk, in the context of scientific research and engineering solutions.
8. The 2021 International Conference on Internet of Things (ICIOT 2021, http://iciot. org/), which addressed the creation of IoT technologies and the development of IOT services.
9. The 2021 International Conference on Edge Computing (EDGE 2021, http://the edgecomputing.org/), which put its focus on the state of the art and practice of edge computing including, but not limited to, localized resource sharing, connections with the cloud, and 5G devices and applications.
10. The 2021 International Conference on Blockchain (ICBC 2021, http://blockc hain1000.org/), which concentrated on blockchain-based services and enabling technologies.

Some of the highlights of SCF 2021 were as follows:

- Bigger Platform: The 10 collocated conferences (SCF 2021) got sponsorship from the Services Society which is the world-leading not-for-profits organization (501 c(3)) dedicated to serving more than 30,000 services computing researchers and practitioners worldwide. A bigger platform means bigger opportunities for all volunteers, authors, and participants. In addition, Springer provided sponsorship for best paper awards and other professional activities. All 10 conference proceedings of SCF 2021 will be published by Springer and indexed in the ISI Conference Proceedings Citation Index (included in the Web of Science), the Engineering Index EI (Compendex and Inspec databases), DBLP, Google Scholar, IO-Port, MathSciNet, Scopus, and ZBlMath.
- Brighter Future: While celebrating the 2021 version of ICWS, SCF 2021 highlighted the Fourth International Conference on Blockchain (ICBC 2021) to build the fundamental infrastructure for enabling secure and trusted services ecosystems. It will also lead our community members to create their own brighter future.
- Better Model: SCF 2021 continued to leverage the invented Conference Blockchain Model (CBM) to innovate the organizing practices for all 10 collocated conferences.

Contents

An Overview of Human Activity Recognition Using Wearable Sensors: Healthcare and Artificial Intelligence

Rex Liu[1], Albara Ah Ramli[1(✉)], Huanle Zhang[1], Erik Henricson[2], and Xin Liu[1]

[1] Department of Computer Science, School of Engineering, University of California, Davis, Davis, USA
{rexliu,arramli,dtczhang,xinliu}@ucdavis.edu
[2] Department of Physical Medicine and Rehabilitation, School of Medicine, University of California, Davis, Davis, USA
ehenricson@ucdavis.edu

Abstract. With the rapid development of the internet of things (IoT) and artificial intelligence (AI) technologies, human activity recognition (HAR) has been applied in a variety of domains such as security and surveillance, human-robot interaction, and entertainment. Even though a number of surveys and review papers have been published, there is a lack of HAR overview papers focusing on healthcare applications that use wearable sensors. Therefore, we fill in the gap by presenting this overview paper. In particular, we present our projects to illustrate the system design of HAR applications for healthcare. Our projects include early mobility identification of human activities for intensive care unit (ICU) patients and gait analysis of Duchenne muscular dystrophy (DMD) patients. We cover essential components of designing HAR systems including sensor factors (e.g., type, number, and placement location), AI model selection (e.g., classical machine learning models versus deep learning models), and feature engineering. In addition, we highlight the challenges of such healthcare-oriented HAR systems and propose several research opportunities for both the medical and the computer science community.

Keywords: Human activity recognition (HAR) · Healthcare · Internet of things (IoT) · Artificial intelligence (AI) · Wearable sensors

1 Introduction

Human activity recognition has been actively researched in the past decade, thanks to the increasing number of deployed smart devices such as smartphones and IoT devices. Based on the type of data being processed, a HAR system can be classified into vision-based and sensor-based. This paper targets wearable-sensor

R. Liu and A. A. Ramli—These two authors contributed equally to this work.

B. Tekinerdogan et al. (Eds.): ICIOT 2021, LNCS 12993, pp. 1–14, 2022.
https://doi.org/10.1007/978-3-030-96068-1_1

HAR systems in healthcare, which are the most prevalent type of sensor-based HAR systems [1]. More importantly, wearable-sensor HAR systems do not suffer from severe privacy issues like vision-based HAR systems, making wearable-sensor HAR systems suitable for healthcare applications. In a wearable-sensor HAR system, a user wears portable mobile devices that have built-in sensors. The user's activities can then be classified by measuring and characterizing sensor signals when the user is conducting daily activities.

HAR for healthcare has many potential use cases, including (1) Moving gait diagnosis from expensive motion labs to the community. Gait analysis can be used in many healthcare applications, such as stroke detection, gait modification (to prevent failing), and certain disease early detection. (2) Cognitive behavior monitoring and intervention for children and adults with attention-deficit/hyperactivity disorder (ADHD). We can leverage sensors to investigate whether fidgeting positively or negatively affects attention. (3) Stroke-patient hospital direction. When a patient is in an ambulance, a life-and-death question is whether the patient has extensive brain hemorrhage. If so, the patient should be directed to a hospital that can treat such cases. UCSF has developed a device based on an accelerometer sensor to help make this critical decision. (4) Epilepsy and Parkinson's disease study. Doctors have collected a significant amount of data on electrophysiology and episodic memory in rodents and human patients. The analysis of such sensing data can be used for various disease identification and treatment purpose. (5) An expensive device, called Vision RT, is used to ensure radiation therapy is delivered safely to cancer patients (due to patient motion). It is worth exploiting sensors to detect the patient's movement while taking radiation therapy for the less affluent communities.

However, building practical wearable-sensor HAR systems for healthcare applications not only has challenges (e.g., sensor setup, data collection, and AI model selection) that are faced by traditional wearable-HAR systems, but also challenges that are unique to the healthcare domain. For example, in addition to the overall AI model accuracy (averaging results of all users), clinicians are concerned about the model stability (i.e., the model has approximately the same accuracy for each user) and model interpretability (e.g., to discover patient movement patterns that are specific to some symptoms).

Therefore, we present this overview paper in the hope to shed light on designing wearable-sensor HAR systems for healthcare applications. To illustrate the system considerations, we share two of our healthcare systems: one for identifying the early mobility activities of ICU patients [2] and the other one for the gait analysis of DMD patients [3]. Our projects demonstrate that HAR systems for healthcare not only have commonalities such as data processing pipelines but also differences in terms of sensor setup and system requirements.

We organize this paper as follows. First, we provide the preliminaries of HAR systems. Next, we introduce our HAR systems for ICU patients and DMD patients. Then, we explain the considerations when designing a HAR system. Last, we highlight the challenges of applying wearable-sensor-based HAR systems to healthcare, and propose several research opportunities. Last, we conclude this paper.

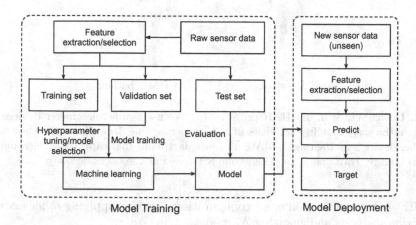

Fig. 1. General data flow for the two-stages of HAR systems: model training and model deployment.

2 Human Activity Recognition: A Primer

Given the short time-length data of wearable sensors, a HAR system needs to recognize the activity from which the data is generated. Thanks to the rapid advancement of AI technology, AI algorithms/models are increasingly adopted for recognizing the activity from the sensor data. Figure 1 illustrates the general data flow for an AI-based HAR system, which can be divided into two stages: model training and model deployment.

In the model training stage, an AI model is trained and tailored for the specific application. To achieve an accurate AI model, the following steps are often applied. First, raw sensor data from different activities should be collected. The quality of collected data significantly affects the AI model performance. The collected data is required to be diverse, representative, and large in the number of samples. Afterward, the raw data is divided into fixed-length or dynamic-length segments (i.e., time windows) [4]. Then, feature extraction is used to extract potentially useful features from the data segmentation, and feature selection is adopted to remove irrelevant features [5]. To alleviate the overfitting problem of the trained model, the set of processed features are divided into a training set, a validation set, and a test set. During the AI model training, we use the training set to tune the AI model and the validation set to measure the model's accuracy. After we finish the model training, we use the test set to evaluate the trained model. The trained model is deployed to real-world applications if its accuracy is satisfactory. Otherwise, the whole model training stage is performed

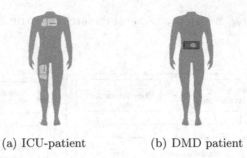

(a) ICU-patient   (b) DMD patient

Fig. 2. Device setups in our HAR projects. (a) We use two accelerometer devices to recognize the early mobility activities of ICU patients. One device is on the chest and the other device is on the thigh. (b) We use one smartphone that captures accelerometer data to identify DMD patients. The phone is located at the backside body.

repetitively by exploring different configurations, such as applying other feature extraction methods and changing AI models.

In the model deployment stage, the same data processing (e.g., segmentation, feature extraction, and selection) is applied to the new and unseen sensor data, and the trained model is executed on the processed data. It is possible that the trained model may not work as expected in a real deployment, probably due to the model over-fitting or the lack of generality in the collected dataset [6]. In this situation, the system designer needs to revert to the model training stage.

3   HAR Applications in Healthcare

Clinicians have already applied wearable sensor-based HAR systems in healthcare, thanks to the development of more lightweight wearable devices, greater computation capability, and higher accurate AI algorithms. This section presents our two HAR healthcare projects to illustrate the considerations when designing HAR systems for healthcare applications with different goals.

3.1   Case 1: Identification of Early Mobility Activity for ICU Patients

Due to long periods of inactivity and immobilization, patients become weak when recovering from major illnesses in ICU [7]. If ICU patients' activities can be accurately recognized, clinicians can provide an optimal personalized dose of mobilities for ICU patients' different illness conditions. Therefore, doctors and researchers are extremely interested in ICU patients' early mobilization, which is an effective and safe intervention to improve functional outcomes [8]. However, early mobility activity (EMA) research is limited by the lack of accurate, effective, and comprehensive methods to recognize patients' activities in ICU.

We propose a wearable sensor-based HAR system for recognizing the EMA of ICU patients [2]. In our system, Each ICU patient wears two accelerometer devices: one on the chest and the other on the thigh, as shown in Fig. 2(a). Each device continuously collects 3-axis accelerometer data at a sampling rate 32 Hz. Figure 3(a) plots the accelerometer data when an ICU patient sits on the cardiac chair to achieve an optimal resting position. This project aims to classify 20 types of ICU-related activities (e.g., reposition, percussion).

This project has two main challenges in designing the HAR system for ICU patients. (1) Label Noise. Because the time lengths for accomplishing an early mobility activity are different for ICU patients with varying health conditions, it is laborious and time-consuming work for clinicians to annotate sensor data for each second in the real world. Therefore, our EMA sensor data are annotated for each minute by a medical expert after data collection. However, one-minute length is exceedingly long for some early mobility activities such as Reposition, which the patient needs less than 20 s to accomplish. This annotation process introduces the label noise in our EMA dataset, which decreases the accuracy of the model. (2) Sensor Orientation. In the actual data collection process and possible future applications, we cannot guarantee that the orientations of all accelerometers are the same, and different orientations of the accelerometers lead to different meanings of XYZ coordinate values. Therefore, without careful feature extraction and selection, the AI model generalizes poorly to different patients, affecting the system performance in practice.

To tackle these challenges and improve the accuracy of recognizing ICU patient's activities, we explore the following techniques. (1) We propose a segment voting process to handle the label noise. Specifically, each one-minute sensor data is divided into multiple fixed half-overlapped sliding segments (time windows). We train our AI model using the segments. To predict each one-minute sensor data activity, we apply our trained model to each segment. The final prediction result for the one-minute data is the activity that has the majority vote among the prediction of all segments. Our segmenting method improves the model accuracy by ∼4.08% and reduces the model instability by ∼9.77% [2]. Our experiments also demonstrate that the number of sensors contributes to eliminating label noise in our dataset. As shown in Fig. 3(a), the increase in the number of sensors conveys more information, and thus improves the system's accuracy. (2) We identify and extract features that are not sensitive to sensor orientations to tackle the sensor orientation problem. Our features improve both the accuracy and the stability of AI models compared to the model trained on commonly used features.

3.2   Case 2: Identification of Gait Characteristics for DMD Patients

Duchenne muscular dystrophy (DMD) is a genetic disorder disease that affects the dystrophin protein, essential for keeping muscle cells intact. It has an estimated incidence of 1:5000 male births, and untreated boys become wheelchair-bound by the age of 12 years and die in their late teens to early 20s [9]. There is presently no cure for DMD disease. Nonetheless, gene repair interventions and other preventive therapies can be initiated as early as possible to slow the disease's progress and prevent secondary conditions. Therefore, it is important

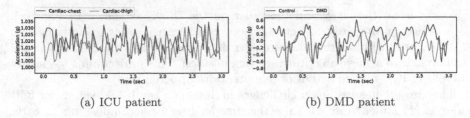

(a) ICU patient   (b) DMD patient

Fig. 3. Illustration of accelerometer data in our projects. (a) The z-axis of the accelerometer data from the two on-body devices when an ICU patient is performing the cardiac activity. (b) The z-axis of the accelerometer data, which shows the difference in gait characteristics between a DMD patient and a healthy person.

to identify children with DMD early in the course of their disease and have tools for quantitative evaluation of their gait in both the clinic and community environments.

We designed a wearable sensor-based HAR system to identify gait characteristics associated with the progression of gait abnormalities in children with DMD and to differentiate those patterns from those of typically developing peers [3, 10] To leverage this idea, we design a HAR system in which we use a smartphone to capture accelerometer data from the participants. As Fig. 2(b) illustrates, participants wear a smartphone at the back of the hips over the spine (lumbosacral junction) at a location that is the closest surface point to the body's center of mass. Each smartphone collects 3-axis accelerometer data at a sampling rate 30 Hz with the same phone orientation.

We recruited ambulatory participants with DMD between 3 and 13 years of age and typically developing controls of similar ages. We ask participants to perform exercises at various times, speeds, and distances such as free walk and 6-minute walk, as specified by the north star ambulatory assessment (NSAA) standard [11]. Figure 3(b) shows the gait pattern difference between a DMD patient and a healthy person when they are walking.

We found that classical machine learning and deep learning, after hyperparameter fine-tuning and cross-validation on seven different gait activities, led to the best performance with an accuracy exceeding 91% on the 6-min-walk-test activity [3]. We demonstrate that by using AI techniques and an accelerometer, we can distinguish between the DMD gait and typically developing peers.

There are two main challenges in designing our HAR system for the DMD application: clinical interpretability and data sparsity. (1) Clinical Interpretability. Medical practitioners desire not only a high prediction accuracy but also an interpretation of the prediction result. (2) Data Sparsity. In the healthcare domain, collecting diverse and sufficient data is challenging, especially for fatal diseases such as DMD.

We explore the following techniques to tackle these challenges. (1) To interpret AI model outcomes, we plan to link the clinical measurements with the model's extracted features by leveraging advanced AI models such as interpretable CNN [12]. However, it is an active, challenging task to find which clinical measurements correlated with the AI model features, especially for deep learning models. (2) To overcome the lack of data, we plan to use Generative Adversarial Network (GAN) [13] or synthetic minority over-sampling technique (SMOTE) [14] to generate more data samples.

3.3 Summary of Our Projects

Our two projects target different healthcare applications with different goals: recognizing ICU patients' activities and distinguishing DMD gait patterns from those typically developing controls. The ICU project focuses on the system performance to assist the doctor in better understanding patients' recovery. While achieving high system performance, the DMD project interprets the model results further and discovers disease-specific patterns to determine the patient's condition and progression. Our example projects demonstrate the effectiveness and potential of wearable sensor-based HAR systems in healthcare. However, due to the different goals, different healthcare applications may have additional HAR system considerations. For example, our two projects adopt a different number of devices (2 versus 1) and device position (chest and thigh versus central mass body). In addition, our projects also apply different feature extractions (time and frequency domain versus clinical). In the next section, we present design considerations for building HAR systems.

4 System Design

This section covers three design considerations essential for HAR systems, i.e., sensor, feature extraction and selection, and AI model selection.

4.1 Sensor

Sensors play an essential role in wearable HAR systems. Different HAR systems adopt various sensor configurations regarding the type of sensors, the sensor position and orientation, and the number of sensors.

Sensor Types. There are several types of sensors. Each sensor captures a different raw movement signal. The most commonly-used wearable sensors in HAR systems are accelerometer, gyroscope, and electrocardiography (ECG). The accelerometer sensor captures the acceleration signal that is useful for recognizing movements such as walking, running, and jumping. Gyroscopes capture the rotation movements used commonly in recognizing swinging, turning, and repositioning. ECG captures the heart rate and rhythm, which helps distinguish between intensive and light exercises.

However, many activities include both directional and rotational movements. Therefore, using one sensor type is not adequate. As a result, multiple types of sensors (e.g., accelerometer and gyroscope) are used in various application scenarios to maximize accuracy. However, using multiple types of sensors is challenging due to the increased complexity of the system in terms of synchronization issues [15].

Sensor Position and Orientation. Different positions and orientations of devices affect the data features and thus the model accuracy in predicting different activities [16]. However, there have not yet been systematic comparisons of the number, type, and location of sensors to determine whether an optimal array design can capture data across a wide range of human activities and disease states. In many cases, the device position and orientation are decided by the empirical experience of clinicians.

Number of Sensors. Generally, a large number of sensors require demanding storage and computation capability. On the other hand, more sensors can collect more diverse data, which is beneficial for improving model performance [17]. Therefore, to decide the optimal number of sensors, researchers need to carefully consider many factors such as cost, power consumption, and accuracy target as well as the feasibility of long-term use in the community to collect real-world information [18].

4.2 Feature Extraction and Selection

In addition to the hardware setup, feature extraction and selection significantly affect the overall system performance. Before applying feature engineering to the data, the input data needs to be segmented.

Data Segmentation. HAR systems collect data constantly via wearable sensors to identify possible activities. Data segmentation is applied to divide comparatively long time data into short fragments (time windows) that are suitable for AI models to learn. There are two types of data segmentation: fixed-length and dynamic-length [4]. For fixed-length segmentation, if the time window is too short, the extracted features from the fragments are insufficient to capture the activity; on the other hand, if the time window is too long, a fragment is likely to contain multiple activities. The system accuracy deteriorates in both cases. In comparison, a dynamic-length data segmentation adopts an adaptive length of fragments corresponding to the characteristics of input data. Ideally, dynamic data segmentation generates fragments, in which each fragment only contains a single and complete activity. However, dynamic data segmentation is much more complex than fixed data segmentation, and thus are not as widely adopted by existing works as fixed-length segmentation.

Feature Extraction. Feature extraction is then applied to extract important features from the data fragments [5]. It can be broadly classified into time-domain and frequency-domain methods. In time-domain feature extraction, metrics such as median, variance, mean, and skewness are calculated over the amplitude variations of data over time. Time-domain features are lightweight to compute and thus are friendly to low-profile embedded devices and real-time applications. In comparison, frequency-domain features calculate the frequency variations of data over time. They include metrics such as spectral entropy, spectral power, and peak frequency. The computation overhead of frequency-domain features is generally much greater than time-domain features. In reality, most existing HAR systems adopt both time-domain features and frequency-domain features, in the consideration of the tradeoff among factors such as system accuracy, computation overhead, and power consumption.

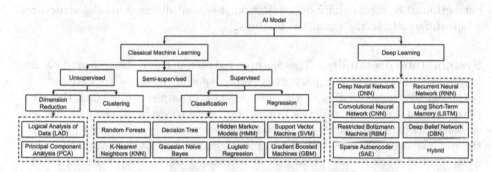

Fig. 4. Classical machine learning and deep learning algorithms used in HAR systems.

Feature Selection. Feature selection is often adopted in order to reduce system complexity. It measures the importance of features and then removes irrelevant features. Feature selection is roughly divided into three methods: filter methods, wrapper methods, and embedded/hybrid methods [5]. Filter methods select a subset of features by exploiting inherent characteristics of features, whereas wrapper methods use classifiers to estimate the useful features. On the other hand, the embedded/hybrid methods combine the results from filter methods and wrapper methods [1]. By carefully selecting features, the AI model accuracy can be significantly improved. However, in healthcare HAR systems, pursuing high accuracy is not the sole goal, as the features are often manually decided by medical experts for identifying patients. Therefore, healthcare HAR systems require feature extraction and selection that is meaningful for clinicians and meanwhile achieves high prediction accuracy.

4.3 AI Model Selection

In the HAR field, classical machine learning algorithms and deep learning algorithms have been explored and applied, which is summarized in Fig. 4. Both classical machine learning algorithms and deep learning algorithms have different advantages and disadvantages.

Dataset Requirement and System Running Overhead. The data collection process in the healthcare scenario is challenging because of the severe privacy issue and rare incidence rate of some medical activities. Therefore, in most healthcare applications, the database size is small. Correspondingly, classical machine learning models are more preferred because they work well with medium-size datasets. In contrast, even though deep learning models achieve better accuracy, they usually require a large amount of data for training. Real-time performance is another critical factor for some healthcare applications [19]. For example, [20] uses cranial accelerometers to detect stroke in an ambulance to decide whether to send the patient to a specialist stroke hospital for special treatment. Therefore, lightweight models are preferred in this use case. In addition to the running overhead of the AI models, the processing time of feature extraction also affects the model selection, because different model structures adapt differently to the extracted features.

System Interpretability. The features extracted from the sensor data are helpful to understand the pattern of some specific diseases to find out the pathological characteristics of the disease. For example, we extract the temporal/spatial gait characteristics from sensor data to evaluate the gait changes associated with DMD. Classical machine learning models are easier to interpret the model's decision, especially in decision tree models. Even though there is a great deal of work in interpreting deep learning models, deep learning models have the reputation of poor interpretability.

5   Challenges and Opportunities

Wearable sensor-based HAR systems are promising for a variety of healthcare problems. However, there are several challenges in fully exploiting them to build satisfactory HAR systems for healthcare. In this section, we identify challenges as well as research opportunities of HAR systems for healthcare.

5.1   Data Sparsity

The most commonly used algorithms for the HAR system in healthcare are the supervised learning algorithms that need extensive labeled data. For some daily living activities such as walking and running, researchers could get a significant amount of the labeled data from the public dataset or the raw sensor data collected and annotated by themselves. However, for some specific human activities related to healthcare, such as the therapeutic activities of patients, researchers could not get enough sensor data since these activities are low-probability events compared with daily life activities. Furthermore, it also takes time and effort to locate the sensor data of these specific activities from the daily data and label them. For example, when patients recover from surgery, they need some range of motion (ROM) exercises several times a day to make their joints and muscles flexible and strong again. Because of the fixed and limited collection times per day and the limited number of patients are involved, raw sensor data for ROM becomes insufficient, affecting the HAR system's performance. Therefore, building HAR systems with high accuracy on small datasets in healthcare is one of the most significant challenges.

Meta-learning is one of the approaches to solve this challenge. Meta-learning aims to optimize models which can learn efficiently in a small dataset when dealing with new categories. In [21], researchers present a meta-learning methodology based on the Model-Agnostic Meta-Learning algorithm [22] to build personal HAR models. In [23], researchers use few-shot learning to transfer information from existing activity recognition models. However, it is unclear whether these techniques work well for medical applications. So more research is needed to explore the feasibility of transferring knowledge from daily living activities to specific activities related to healthcare.

5.2   Model Interpretability

In HAR applications in healthcare, an increasing number of applications focus on the interpretability of the model to extract relevant features, in order to describe the severity of the disease and track the progression of the disease [3]. In addition, notwithstanding the benefit of deep learning in HAR, the underlying mechanics of machine learning are still unclear. So, various studies are trying to explain the deep learning model for the recognition of human activities. The common approach to interpreting the deep learning model is to compute the importance of each part of the input. In [24], researchers propose an interpretable convolutional neural network to select the most important sensor position for some specific activities. Instead of computing the importance of each part of the input, another approach is to make a sequence of selections about which part of the input is essential for the model training [25]. More research is required to adopt these methods to HAR systems for healthcare.

5.3   Concurrent Activities

Most of the existing HAR research focuses on single-labeled activity, recognizing only one activity of the given data segment. However, in real-world healthcare scenarios, humans can perform multiple activities concurrently. For example, patients can do ROM exercises and percussion therapy at the same time. The AI model performance deteriorates for concurrent activities. On the other hand, designing models to recognize multiple activities per data segment is a challenging task.

5.4   Composite Activities

In healthcare applications, optimizing HAR algorithms to identify composite activities in the community is ultimately more desirable than recognizing a single type of task. For example, when a patient moves from bed to the chair, the patient performs various activities, including sitting from supine in the bed, pivoting to place feet on the floor, standing from sitting, walking a few steps, and then sitting down on a chair. Therefore, it is preferred that an AI model can directly recognize the composite activity.

5.5 Privacy

Wearable sensor-based HAR systems do not suffer from severe privacy issues as camera-based vision systems. However, since HAR applications continuously capture user data and recognize user activities, they may leak users' personal information if data are not secured. Therefore, secure data sharing and safe data storage are imperative for healthcare applications. To alleviate sensitive information during model training, adversarial loss functions are leveraged to guard against privacy leakage [26]. In addition, federated learning is a promising solution, which trains a global model without exposing local devices' private data [27].

5.6 Opportunities of HAR for Healthcare

Through our experience with HAR systems for healthcare, we identify the following research opportunities.

- **Community-based healthcare**. Community-based healthcare requires that user devices are lightweight and affordable for the public. In addition, instructing the non-expert users/patients should be straightforward to follow. We can use digital sensing capability and the popularity of mobile devices to enable large community-based prescreening for various diseases and early signs of diseases. This can be done in a privacy-preserving manner in the sense that data does not need to leave a local device if necessary. For example, our DMD project enables community-based diagnosis during the pandemic and in rural areas where specialty labs are hundreds of miles away.
- **Chronic disease prevention and intervention.** For chronic diseases, it is essential to capture the behaviors of patients in the long run. To this end, gait analysis, motion monitoring, ECG, and other vital signals (such as continuous glucose monitoring) can play a key role.
- **Health aging**. With the decreased fertility rates and the increased life expectancy, population aging is becoming common for most countries. Therefore, building HAR systems for healthy aging is beneficial for senior citizens and society as a whole. We anticipate that gait and motion monitoring and diagnosis will play a critical role in healthy aging.

6   Conclusion

It is gaining popularity by applying wearable sensors to recognize and analyze human activities for the healthcare domain. For example, we leverage HAR systems to recognizing patients' early mobility activities in ICU and to analyzing the symptoms of DMD patients. This overview paper covers the system design of HAR systems based on wearable sensors, focusing on healthcare applications. We emphasize the essential components of HAR systems, including sensor factors, data segmentation, feature extraction and selection, and AI model comparison. We also highlight the challenges and opportunities of HAR systems for healthcare.

References

1. Dang, L.M., Min, K., Wang, H., Jalil Piran, Md., Lee, C.H., Moon, H.: Sensor-based and vision-based human activity recognition: a comprehensive survey. Pattern Recognit. **108**, 1–41 (2020)
2. Liu, R., Fazio, S.A., Zhang, H., Ramli, A.A., Liu, X., Adams, J.Y.: Early mobility recognition for intensive care unit patients using accelerometers. In: KDD Workshop on Artificial Intelligence of Things (AIoT), pp. 1–6 (2021)
3. Ramli, A.A., et al.: Gait characterization in Duchenne muscular dystrophy (DMD) using a single-sensor accelerometer: classical machine learning and deep learning approaches (2021)
4. Noor, M.H.M., Salcic, Z., Wang, K.I.-K.: Adaptive sliding window segmentation for physical activity recognition using a single tri-axial accelerometer. Pervasive Mob. Comput. **38**(1), 41–59 (2016)
5. Khalid, S., Khalil, T., Nasreen, S.: A survey of feature selection and feature extraction techniques in machine learning. In: Science and Information Conference, pp. 372–378 (2014)
6. Wang, J., Chen, Y., Hao, S., Peng, X., Lisha, H.: Deep learning for sensor-based activity recognition: a survey. Pattern Recogn. Lett. **119**, 3–11 (2019)
7. Castro-Avila, A.C., Seron, P., Fang, E., Gaete, M., Mickan, S.: Effect of early rehabilitation during intensive care unit stay on functional status: systematic review and meta-analysis. PLoS ONE **10**(7), 1–21 (2015)
8. Adler, J., Malone, D.: Early mobilization in the intensive care unit: a systematic review. Cardiopulm. Phys. Ther. J. **23**, 5–13 (2012)
9. Yiu, E.M., Kornberg, A.J.: Duchenne muscular dystrophy. J. Paediatr. Child Health **51**, 759–764 (2015)
10. Ramli, A.A., et al.: An automated system for early diagnosis, severity, and progression identification in duchenne muscular dystrophy: a machine learning and deep learning approach. In: Annual Human Genomics Symposium - University of California Davis Medical Center, p. 12 (2020)
11. Physiopedia: North start ambulatory assessment. https://www.physio-pedia.com/North_Star_Ambulatory_Assessment. Accessed 29 June 2021
12. Zhang, Q., Wu, Y.N., Zhu, S.-C.: Interpretable convolutional neural networks. In: IEEE/CVF Conference on Computer Vision and Pattern Recognition (CVPR), pp. 8827–8836 (2018)
13. Goodfellow, I.J., et al.: Generative adversarial networks (2014). arXiv:1406.2661
14. Chawla, N.V., Bowyer, K.W., Hall, L.O., Kegelmeyer, W.P.: Smote: synthetic minority over-sampling technique. J. Artif. Intell. Res. **16**(1), 321–357 (2002)
15. Lara, O.D., Labrador, M.A.: A survey on human activity recognition using wearable sensors. IEEE Commun. Surv. Tutor. **15**(3), 1192–1209 (2013)

16. Maurer, U., Smailagic, A., Siewiorek, D.P., Deisher, M.: Activity recognition and monitoring using multiple sensors on different body positions. In: International Workshop on Wearable and Implantable Body Sensor Networks (BSN), pp. 1–4 (2006)
17. Van Laerhoven, K., Schmidt, A., Gellersen, H.-W.: Multi-sensor context aware clothing. In: International Symposium on Wearable Computers, pp. 1–8 (2002)
18. Jarchi, D., Pope, J., Lee, T.K.M., Tamjidi, L., Mirzaei, A., Sanei, S.: A review on accelerometry-based gait analysis and emerging clinical applications. IEEE Rev. Biomed. Eng. **11**, 177–194 (2018)
19. Ramli, A.A., et al.: BWCNN: blink to word, a real-time convolutional neural network approach. In: Song, W., Lee, K., Yan, Z., Zhang, L.-J., Chen, H. (eds.) ICIOT 2020. LNCS, vol. 12405, pp. 133–140. Springer, Cham (2020). https://doi.org/10. 1007/978-3-030-59615-6_10
20. Keenan, K., Lovoi, P., Smith, W.: The neurological examination improves cranial accelerometry large vessel occlusion prediction accuracy. Neurocrit. Care **35**, 1–10 (2020)
21. Wijekoon, A., Wiratunga, N.: Learning-to-learn personalised human activity recognition models (2020). arXiv:2006.07472
22. Finn, C., Abbeel, P., Levine, S.: Model-agnostic meta-learning for fast adaptation of deep networks. In: Proceedings of the 34th International Conference on Machine Learning, pp. 1126–1135 (2017)
23. Feng, S., Duarte, M.: Few-shot learning-based human activity recognition. Expert Syst. Appl. **138**, 1–12 (2019)
24. Kim, E.: Interpretable and accurate convolutional neural networks for human activity recognition. IEEE Trans. Industr. Inf. **16**(11), 7190–7198 (2020)
25. Chen, K., et al.: Interpretable parallel recurrent neural networks with convolutional attentions for multi-modality activity modeling (2018). arXiv:1805.07233
26. Iwasawa, Y., Nakayama, K., Yairi, I., Matsuo, Y.: Privacy issues regarding the application of DNNs to activity-recognition using wearables and its countermeasures by use of adversarial training. In: International Joint Conference on Artificial Intelligence (IJCAI), pp. 1930–1936 (2017)
27. McMahan, H.B., Moore, E., Ramage, D., Hampson, S., Arcas, B.A.: Communication-efficient learning of deep networks from decentralized data. In: International Conference on Artificial Intelligence and Statistics (AISTATS), pp. 1–10 (2017)

Risks and Challenges of Training Classifiers for IoT

Franck Le[✉], Seraphin Calo, and Dinesh Verma

IBM T.J. Watson Research Center, New York, US
{fle,scalo,dverma}@us.ibm.com

Abstract. Although deep learning algorithms can achieve high performance, deep models may not learn the right concepts and can easily overfit their training datasets. In the context of IoT devices, the problem is further exacerbated by three factors. First, traffic may be encrypted, allowing very little visibility into the activity of the endpoints. Second, devices with different models and manufacturers may exhibit very different behaviors. Finally, contrary to domains like computer vision or natural language processing, there is no well-accepted representation for the network data that characterizes IoT devices. In this work, we capture real network traffic from different environments, and we demonstrate that training models to detect specific classes of IoT devices (e.g., cameras) using state-of-the-art techniques can lead to overfitting, and very poor performance on independent datasets. However, we then show that by applying domain knowledge, one can manually define engineered features and train simple models (e.g., a decision tree) that achieve an F-1 score of 0.956 on an independent dataset. These results show the feasibility of training generalizable models, but at the same time, raise questions on how best to transform and represent the raw network data to train classifiers for other classes of IoT devices (e.g., hubs, motion sensors) while minimizing manual feature engineering. We elaborate on the challenges, drawing analogies with other fields such as natural language processing.

1 Introduction

Can we train classifiers for classes of IoT devices (e.g., cameras, motion sensors, etc.) that are not specific to the IoT devices present in the training dataset, but that are more general and can identify those with different software versions, firmware versions, or from other models and manufacturers?

This question is motivated by the continuous penetration of IoT products in enterprise environments. Although the Internet of Things (IoT) extends Internet connectivity to a wide range of objects (e.g., from smart electronic appliances to industrial sensors) offering increased efficiency and productivity, it also introduces new challenges to IT departments. More specifically, with their poor security [1–3], IoT devices can constitute a prime target for attacks, e.g., as ingress points to a broader IT infrastructure. In addition, the existence of certain classes of IoT devices in their IT environment (e.g., cameras, audio speakers) may violate company policies. For those reasons, a number of approaches have recently been developed to discover IoT devices through passive network monitoring (e.g., [4–11]), so prohibited devices, and devices susceptible to compromise, can have their network access restricted. For example, Guo and Heidemann [7]

© Springer Nature Switzerland AG 2022
B. Tekinerdogan et al. (Eds.): ICIOT 2021, LNCS 12993, pp. 15–28, 2022.
https://doi.org/10.1007/978-3-030-96068-1_2

exploit the observation that IoT devices often exchange traffic with servers run by their manufacturers. However, network administrators want to discover IoT devices, not only from the same manufacturers than those present in the training dataset, but also from other manufacturers as new IoT products are continuously introduced into the market. More specifically, a network administrator may acquire a number of cameras, e.g., from Dropcam, Insteon, Netatmo, Samsung, TP Link, Withings [4], to train a classifier for cameras. However, the network administrator wants to discover cameras in his network, not only from those manufacturers, but also from other vendors (e.g., Belkin, Foscam, Vera, Zmodo, etc.)

In this paper, we seek to address that challenge. When faced with a classification task, a common approach consists of applying state-of-the-art techniques such as BERT-based models [12–14] for text, or gradient boosted decision trees (GBDT) [15–17] for tabular data. In our case, the input data consists of network traffic, and popular network traffic analyzer tools such as Zeek [18] can process such data formats and extract records for every connection seen in the trace along with the requested HTTP URIs, key headers, MIME types, server responses, DNS requests with replies, SSL certificates, and other key information. As such, the input to the classifier(s) consists of tabular data (where each record represents a connection); and, because GBDTs have been dominating competitions for such a data format, we train a GBDT model to identify cameras using real traces from IoT devices. The classifier achieves a F1 score of 0.910 on the test dataset created using a 80:20 split of the initial records. However, when applying the classifier to the network trace of a new independent network trace comprising cameras from the same and new manufacturers, the classifier performs poorly, achieving a F1 score of 0.281. For the cameras from manufacturers not present in the training dataset, the classifier fails to identify any true positive. In summary, simply applying state-of-the-art techniques resulted in classifiers that perform very well in train-test split evaluation, but fail to generalize to new independent datasets. A closer inspection of the model indeed reveals that the model did not learn the right concepts, but over-fitted the training data.

To address those limitations, we then adopted a different approach that is guided by domain knowledge. More specifically, applying domain knowledge – i.e., knowledge about how IoT devices (e.g., cameras) operate – we defined and created new features and a different representation of the data, and we show that with even only two to three features, a simple decision tree can achieve a F1 score of 0.956 for identifying cameras in the new independent dataset. The results emphasize the importance of domain knowledge, and raise questions on identifying a suitable representation of network data on which general machine learning can be applied. For example, while word embeddings provide a general representation for words and have enabled important breakthroughs in Natural Language Processing, what would be the equivalent of word embeddings for network data?

2   Background

2.1   Packet CAPture (PCAP)

All the information (e.g., email, image, video, software updates) exchanged over the Internet is broken down into packets, which are the basic unit of transport over networks, and essentially consist of a sequence of bytes (1's and 0's). More specifically, packets can be further decomposed into two parts: headers, and body. To explain their roles, an analogy between packets and postal letters is often drawn. A packet header can be compared to the envelope of a letter: It contains metadata of the packet, such as the sender and receiver addresses, as well as other information that describes the packet (e.g., timestamp, sequence numbers to ensure packets arrive in the correct order), but is not the actual data the sender wants to transmit to the receiver. In contrast, the packet body can be compared to the actual letter, and is the data the sender wants to transmit to the receiver. Packet sniffers can capture and record packets from an interface into a file, usually with a .pcap extension, which can subsequently be read and analyzed with network packet analyzers such as Wireshark or tcpdump.

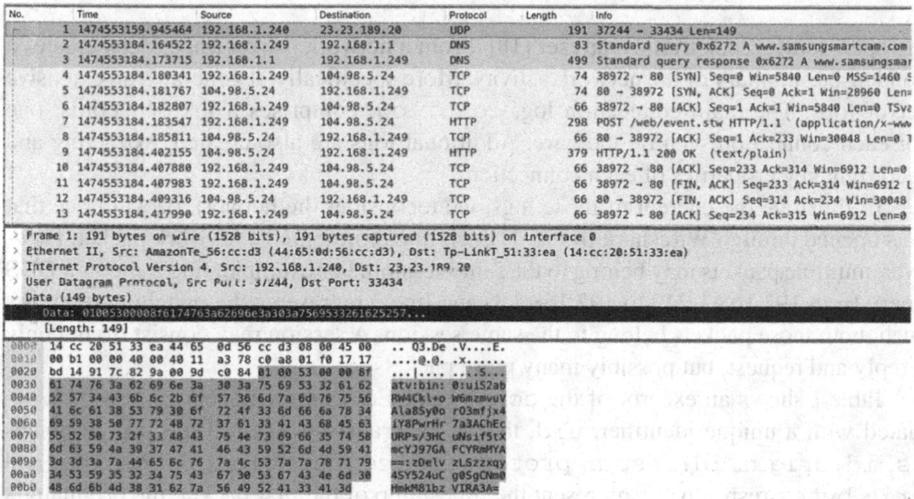

Fig. 1. Wireshark view

Figure 1 represents a view of the Wireshark output on a .pcap file [4]. Each line from the top section represents a packet. The middle section of the Figure expands on the first packet describing the header (e.g., IP, TCP) and the body (also commonly called payload). In particular, the end point at IP address 192.168.1.240 is sending the packet to the end point at IP address 23.23.189.20, and the payload consists of the sequence of bytes starting with "01 00 53" and ending with "33 41 3d". Finally, the bottom section of the Figure represents the packet in hexadecimal format as it is typically sent over the network.

2.2 Zeek

In addition to basic network traffic analyzers such as Wireshark, and tcpdump, that allow one to read network packet traces, a number of more advanced network traffic analyzers have also been developed. In this section, we provide a brief overview of

Table 1. Zeek `conn.log`

ts	uid	id.orig_h	id.resp_h	Proto	Service	Duration	orig_pkts	orig_bytes	...
1474553184.164522	CZfP8R2qX0kHZoYNFe	192.168.1.249	192.168.1.1	udp	dns	0.009193	1	69	...
1474553184.180341	CRKXOUpV9J0ooLc82	192.168.1.249	104.98.5.24	tcp	http	0.228975	6	552	...
...	...	...	...	...	...	...	...	...	...

Table 2. Zeek `dns.log`

...	uid	rtt	Query	Answers	...
...	CZfP8R2qX0kHZoYNFe	0.009193	www.samsungsmartcam.com	www.samsungsmartcam.com.edgekey.net, e6081.b.akamaiedge.net, 104.98.5.24	...
...	...	...	...	...	...

the open-source Zeek traffic analyzer [18]. From a network packet trace, Zeek creates a condensed summary of the network activity. More specifically, it generates an extensive set of logs. The main connection log, `conn.log`, comprises a list of records, one for each connection seen on the wire. Additional logs are also created, extracting and recording key properties of each connection.

To illustrate the content of those logs, we reconsider the network packet trace that was opened through Wireshark in Fig. 1. Each line represented a network packet. However, multiple packets may belong to the same session. For example, line 2 shows a DNS query from 192.168.1.249 to 192.168.1.1, and line 3 represents the matching reply. As such, both those packets belong to the same session. A session may consist of, not only a reply and request, but possibly many more packets.

Table 1 shows an excerpt of the `conn.log`: Each line represents a session associated with a unique identifier, `uid`, that is generated by Zeek. The other attributes `ts`, `id.orig_h`, `id.resp_h`, `proto`, `service`, `duration`, `orig_pkts`, and `orig_bytes` respectively, represent the timestamp of the first packet, the originator's IP address, the responder's IP address, the transport layer protocol, the application protocol, the duration of the connection, the number of packets the originator sent, and the number of bytes the originator sent, respectively. The actual `conn.log` contains a longer list of attributes; and the first line of Table 1 corresponds to the DNS exchange in lines 2 and 3 from Fig. 1. Because this session consists of a DNS (service) exchange, additional attributes that are specific to the DNS protocol are also extracted and recorded in the Zeek `dns.log`.

Table 2 provides an excerpt of the `dns.log`. Each record corresponds to a DNS exchange, and can be matched to the records in `conn.log` thanks to the `uid`. In particular, the first record corresponds to the previous DNS exchange (line 2 in Table 1). The `dns.log` extracts further details that are DNS specific. For example, it reveals that the originator queried for "www.samsungsmartcam.com" and received the following list as reply "[www.samsungsmartcam.com.edgekey.net, e6081.b.akamaiedge.net, 104.98.5.24]". In summary, Zeek processes a network packet trace, reconstructs sessions from the network packets, and extracts key attributes for each session in tabular format. For further details, we refer readers to the Zeek documentation [18].

Table 3. Datasets

Name	Dataset 1	Dataset 2	Dataset 3	Dataset 4
Source	Public [4]	Private	Private	Private
Number of cameras	7	11	5	114
Number of other devices	15	54	34	149
Year of capture	2016	2017	2019	2020
Duration of capture (days)	19	30	1	1

2.3 Gradient Boosted Decision Tree (GBDT)

Gradient-boosted decision trees [15–17] have been dominating competitions for tabular data [19,20], and in this section, we provide a brief background on those models, .e.g., what the main idea is, and how they are trained.

Gradient boosting trains an ensemble of decision trees to predict a target label. However, in contrast to bagging and random forests – where a number of decision trees are built independently and in parallel by taking samples with replacement, and then individual outcomes are finally combined by majority voting – the decision trees are trained and added sequentially to minimize the error from the previous trees. More specifically, decision trees are trained to predict the residuals where a residual is the difference between the actual value and the predicted value. The predicted residuals are then added to the previous predictions to obtain the final classification. Gradient boosted-decision trees are at the core of the XGBoost [19], LightGBM [20] and CatBoost [16] libraries.

3 Objective and Datasets

The goal of this paper is to investigate whether we can train a classifier for classes of IoT devices such that the model is not specific to the training dataset, but can also classify instances that may be coming from different environments, and recognize devices with different software/firmware versions, and from different models/manufacturers. For the purpose of the evaluation and motivated by our internal discussions with network administrators, we focus on binary classifiers for cameras.

Our datasets consist of network packet traces from four independent environments. In each environment, similar to the setting described in [4], a number of IoT devices (both cameras, and non-cameras) were acquired and deployed, and their traffic was captured using `tcpdump`. The number of cameras/non-cameras, the length of the packet captures, and other properties of the datasets are presented in Table 3. To assess the generalization performance of the trained models, we train them using only a subset of the first three datasets, and use the last dataset as the validation dataset. The validation dataset contains both cameras from the same manufacturers as those in the training datasets, and cameras from different manufacturers than those in the training datasets.

4 Blind Learning Approach with State-of-the-Art Techniques

In this first approach, we train the model "blindly", without applying expert knowledge, but by adopting state-of-the-art techniques. More specifically, first, we convert the input packet capture trace into tabular form using an advanced network traffic analyzer (e.g., Zeek) (Sect. 4.1). Second, we train a gradient boosted decision tree model to identify cameras (Sect. 4.2). Then, we validate the model on an independent dataset (Sect. 4.3). Although the model performs well on the training and testing datasets, it performs poorly on the independent validation dataset. The results indicate that the model does not generalize, and we analyze the reasons for this.

4.1 Pre-processing

Records. The raw input data consists of packet capture traces. As described in Sect. 2.1, a packet consists of a sequence of bytes; and multiple packets may belong to a same connection. In addition, because the bytes also encode the protocols (e.g., IP, TCP/UDP, etc.) dictating aspects of the data communication between the originator and the receiver, we apply Zeek, a popular advanced network traffic analyzer, to reconstruct the connections, and extract key properties of the connections. More specifically, Zeek converts a network packet capture into a set of records. Each record corresponds to a connection, and captures key properties of that connection. The number of properties (i.e., attributes) vary depending on the protocols used by the devices. For example, if a device communicates with a server through a protocol that is unknown to Zeek, Zeek can parse and extract only a limited set of features (e.g., number of packets, duration of the connection). In contrast, if Zeek understands and has a parser for the protocol being used (e.g., HTTP), then Zeek can extract a richer set of attributes (e.g., host, method, user agent). We convert and replace missing values in each record with the values of '−1', 0, 'NULL', respectively for Boolean, integer/float, and string attributes, respectively. For attributes that consist of a list, we randomly select one element from the list. Finally, we label each connection with a value of 1 if the originator of the connection is a camera, and 0 otherwise.

Attributes. In addition to the attributes extracted by Zeek, we augment the records with a new attribute called dst_fqdn: Each connection to a server is typically preceded by a DNS exchange. More specifically, a client would have a fully qualified domain name (fqdn), e.g., updates.netgear.com, that is a domain name for a specific service. The client would send a DNS reply for the fqdn and receives a list of IP addresses in return. Those IP addresses represent servers that provide the requested service. Depending on the geographic location of the client (e.g., East versus West coast of the US), the list of IP addresses may differ to allow for load balancing. As such, given a record (i.e., connection), the dst_fqdn represents the fqdn of the service that the client initially requested. To retrieve it, we analyze the DNS traffic from that client and find a fqdn whose list of returned IP addresses match the destination IP address of that record. The reason for adding that attribute is that dst_fqdn may allow better generalization whereas destination ip addresses may be very specific to locations. Finally, we drop attributes that are unique to the devices in the training datasets (e.g., source ip addresses) and that may lead the model to memorize rather than to learn.

Connections. We focus on UDP and TCP connections that are successfully established and terminated, and ignore other connections that are not conducive to the classification tasks: For example, we discard ICMP traffic as this protocol is mainly intended to diagnose network communication issues. Table 4 shows the number of records and attributes for each dataset.

Table 4. Number of records, and attributes for each dataset

Dataset	Dataset 1	Dataset 2	Dataset 3	Dataset 4
Number of records	157,152	1,685,745	443,005	624,355
Number of attributes	80	94	51	139

4.2 Training

We train a gradient boosted decision tree model to classify the records. We selected this specific type of model because after the pre-processing by the Zeek network traffic analyzer, the input data consists of tabular data; and gradient boosted decision trees have been dominating competitions where data is in tabular form.

We merge the records from the first three datasets, and focus on the 47 attributes that are common across all those three datasets. We then split the records into training and testing datasets according to a 80:20 ratio. For the GBDT model, we relied on the CatBoost [16] library and set the number of trees, the depth of the trees, and the loss function to 8, 4, and Logloss. Table 5 reports the F-1 scores: In particular, the model achieves good performance, exceeding 0.910 on the testing dataset.

Table 5. F-1 score of GBDT model on training and testing datasets

Iteration	Training	Testing
0	0.550	0.544
1	0.797	0.798
2	0.790	0.789
3	0.807	0.806
4	0.841	0.871
5	0.871	0.871
6	0.887	0.888
7	0.909	0.910

In addition to allowing one to train a GBDT model, the CatBoost library also offers APIs to analyze the feature importance. More specifically, after perturbing the value of each feature, it inspects the change in predictions. The larger the change, the more important a feature is quantified to be. The importance values are normalized so that the sum of importances of all features equals to 100. Table 6 shows the top 5 features with the highest importance on the training dataset.

Table 6. Top 5 features that are most important on the training dataset

Feature	Importance value
dst_fqdn	27.33
dns_trans_id	13.57
http_host	13.48
dns_qtype_name	7.87
conn_resp_ip_bytes	5.54

1. dst_fqdn represents the fully qualified domain name of the destination IP address. It is extracted by analyzing the DNS traffic. This attribute receives 27% of the importance. This result is in line with previous studies (e.g., [21]) which demonstrated that the fqdn of the destination server can reveal information about the end points. Intuitively, a client establishing a connection with the server www.samsungsmartcam.com is probably a Samsung camera.
2. dns_trans_id is a 16 bit identifier assigned by the client, and used as part of the DNS protocol to match query and response. More specifically, this identifier is copied by the DNS server in the reply and then used by the client to match replies to outstanding queries. This attribute being the second most important feature is unexpected and may suggest that the model memorized, or overfitted, the training dataset.
3. http_host specifies the Internet host of the resource being requested. In other words, this information is similar to the first attribute, dst_fqdn, but is part of HTTP queries. For example, a client sending a HTTP request to the HTTP host www.samsungsmartcam.com is probably a Samsung camera.
4. dns_qtype_name is specific to the DNS protocol, and indicates the type of the DNS resource record. For example, it specifies whether the reply is an IPv4 address, or IPv6 address, etc. This feature suggests that the model may be memorizing or overfitting the training dataset.
5. conn_resp_ip_bytes is the number of bytes the server sent to the client over that connection.

In summary, the trained GBDT model achieves good performance on the testing set (F-1 score > 0.910); and an analysis of the feature importances reveal that while some attributes might suggest potential memorizing or overfitting, the most important features (e.g., dst_fqdn, and http_host) hold out hopes for reasonable generalization performance.

4.3 Validation

After having trained a GBDT model that achieves good performance on a 80:20 validation approach, we evaluate its generalization performance by applying the model to an independent dataset, Dataset 4.

Table 7 presents the F-1 score, precision, and recall of the GBDT model on the independent dataset: The model performs poorly with a F-1 score of 0.281, and a recall

Table 7. Performance of GBDT model on independent dataset

Metric	Value
F-1	0.281
Precision	0.709
Recall	0.175

of 0.175. In other words, many instances that are labelled as "cameras" are classified as "non-cameras".

To understand the reasons for the poor performance, we first look at cameras in the independent dataset from manufacturers that were also present in the training dataset. For example, both the training and independent datasets contain cameras from the manufacturer *foscam*. Focusing on those instances, the GBDT model achieves a precision, recall, and F-1 score, of 1.000, 0.512, and 0.678, respectively. We look at instances that are correctly classified as "cameras", and an analysis of the feature importances assigns 99% of the importance to the attribute dst_fqdn. More specifically, instances from that manufacturer that are correctly classified as "cameras" have two values for this attribute: *time.windows.com*, and *time.nist.gov*. In other words, the model learned that if a device connects to either the server *time.windows.com*, or the server *time.nist.gov*, then the device is a camera. However, this is clearly incorrect: The fqdn *time.windows.com* suggests that the first server is a time server for clients running the Windows operating system to synchronize their time; and the fqdn *time.nist.gov* points to a publicly available cluster of time servers run by the National Institute of Standards and Technology to which any device can connect to synchronize its time [22]. Second, we then look at cameras from manufacturers that were not present in the training datasets. For those instances, the model does not identify any true positive, explaining the poor recall performance. This further demonstrates that the model did not learn the correct concepts.

5 Expert-Guided Learning Approach

The previous section showed that blindly applying state-of-the-art techniques (e.g., Zeek, GBDT) can lead models to achieve good performance on training/testing split evaluation, but very poor results on independent datasets as the models might not learn the right concepts, but may simply over-fit the training data. As such, in this Section, we investigate if guided by domain knowledge, we can obtain better models.

5.1 Pre-processing

Goal. From a network packet trace, what representation should be created for the data to be fed to the machine learning models?

Limitations. Earlier sections relied on advanced network analyzers to convert packet traces into tabular form. More specifically, each record corresponds to a connection.

Then, given a record, the goal of the model consists in determining whether the connection was originated by a camera. However, previous evaluation revealed that many connections may be generic: Cameras and non-cameras may for example need to connect to Internet time servers to synchronize their time. Even domain experts may not be able to distinguish whether such connections were originated by cameras or not. Given these limitations, we propose a different representation.

Solution. Guided by domain knowledge, Internet cameras are expected to present three characteristics. First, they are expected to have a larger average upload rate than other devices (e.g., hubs, printers) which instead may be characterized by larger download rather than upload rates. Second, since cameras stream videos, they may present low burstiness. This is in contrast to devices that may periodically backup data: although those devices may present large uploads, the communications may be characterized by large amount of data sent in shorter times. Finally, earlier studies revealed that IoT devices tend to connect to a low number of remote servers [4].

Based on those insights, we create records as follows. For each device, we focus on its traffic over a configurable period of time (e.g., 24 h). During that time, we extract three features: (1) the average upload rate, (2) the burtiness, and (3) the number of distinct Internet endpoints the device connects to. More specifically, to quantify the level of burtiness, we first compute the average upload rate of every 5 s interval, and then, we calculate their standard deviation.

5.2 Training

We select to train decision trees due to their simplicity and high interpretability. We merge the records from the first two datasets, and obtain 1336 records labeled "non-cameras", and 308 records labeled "cameras". Figure 2 illustrates those records. Each axis represents one feature. The axis labeled "Mean" corresponds to the average upload rate, and the unit is in bits per second.

We balance the dataset by down-sampling, and split it into training:testing datasets according to a 90:10 ratio. Table 8 shows the F-1 score on the training dataset, as we vary the depth of the tree, and Fig. 3 illustrates the decision tree. The model learns that if the number of Internet servers is low, and the average upload rate is high, then the device is a camera. Also, if the number of Internet servers, the average upload rate, and the level of burstiness are all low, then the device is a camera. All those rules are in line with domain knowledge.

Table 8. Performance of decision trees on training dataset

Depth	F-1 score
1	0.776
2	0.776
3	0.690
4	0.810

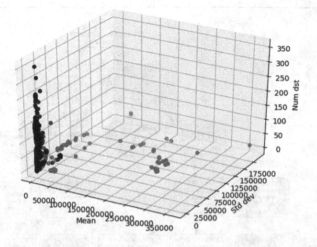

Fig. 2. Representation of the non camera (black) and camera (red) records

5.3 Validation

We evaluate the generalization performance of the decision tree on the independent dataset, Dataset 4. Table 9 summarizes the performance results. First, the decision tree achieves much higher performance (e.g., F-1 score) than the GBDT model, and the performance on the independent dataset is on par with that on the training dataset. Second, as the depth of the tree increases, the F-1 score can decrease because of the risks of overfitting. The depths of 1 and 2 provide the best results. Finally, while the decision tree achieves a recall of 0.942, the precision is lower at 0.636. To better understand the results, we inspect the false positives more closely. A number of records are classified as "camera", but the labels indicate "non camera". Many of those records are actually originated by devices that do comprise a camera. For example, the Chamberlain B4545 Garage Opener is labeled as "non camera" (since it is a garage opener), but its online documentation indicates that it does include a camera: Its *"Integrated video camera enables you to see what is happening in your garage through a live feed or recorded event."* [23]. Similarly, the Nest Hello and Ring Pro doorbells are labeled as "non camera" since they consist of doorbells, but those devices do comprise cameras. As another example, the Night Owl DVR-XHD50B-41, the Lorex LH050400, or the Swann DVR-4600 are all security systems which also include cameras. As such, although the labels did not specify "camera", camera is a feature of those systems, and the model did correctly identify it. Revising and correcting those records result in an actual F-1 score on the independent dataset of 0.956.

6 Discussion

Previous sections demonstrated that it is possible to train a classifier to detect cameras, and that the model can achieve good performance on independent datasets. In fact, the model can consist of a simple decision tree with only three engineered features.

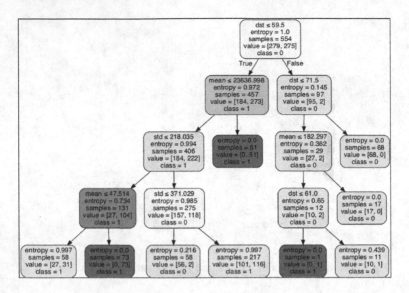

Fig. 3. Illustration of decision tree

Table 9. Performance of decision trees on independent dataset

	Depth 1	Depth 2	Depth 3	Depth 4
Precision	0.636	0.636	0.444	0.617
Recall	0.942	0.942	0.153	0.807
F-1 score	0.759	0.759	0.227	0.699

However, how can the approach generalize to other classes of IoT devices? For example, what representation and features should one select to detect, not cameras, but hubs, motion sensors, or other classes?

We argue that defining a general and suitable representation of network data is key. To draw an analogy with natural language processing, word embeddings have provided a fundamental representation of text, and allowed deep learning models to be successfully trained for a wide range of tasks (e.g., sentence classification, question answering, language modeling, etc.) However, can we identify and define a similar representation for network data?

While network data presents similarities with text, they also present profound differences. For example, text can be viewed as sequences of characters. Similarly, network data can be viewed as sequences of bytes. However, network data also presents unique challenges.

1. **Token** What is the definition of a token in network traffic analysis? In general, a token is an object. For example, in text, words are often considered for tokens, and embeddings are created for each word. Also, words can be identified through clear delimiters such as white spaces. However, what would a token consist of in

network? Also, although network data consists of a stream of bytes, there are no clear delimiters such as white spaces.

2. **Start and end** What should the start and the end of an instance be? In natural language processing, a text (e.g., movie or product review) may represent an instance to be classified. A text is further composed of a sequence of a sentences, each ending with a period or some punctuation (e.g., question mark). However, network data may be continuous with no obvious start and end. A network packet or network connection has a clear beginning and termination, but those may be artifacts of the underlying network medium and protocols. For example, Ethernet may restrict the maximum packet size to be 1500 bytes. Also, as illustrated in Sect. 4, a network connection may not be a suitable representation as different devices may issue very similar connections (e.g., to Internet time servers).

3. **Concurrent connections** Further complicating the problem, although a device may be sending and/or receiving a stream of bytes, those bytes may correspond to multiple connections or to the same or different endpoints.

4. **Encryption** Network data may also be encrypted. Although the header and some information (e.g., public certificates) may still be in cleartext, the payload may be encoded, hiding the information's true meaning.

7 Conclusion

We explored the feasibility of training a classifier for classes of IoT devices that can detect instances from different models and manufacturers than those present in their training dataset. First, we demonstrated that applying state-of-the-art techniques may achieve good performance on 80:20 split evaluation, but achieve poor results on independent datasets due to over-fitting, confirming the research problem. Second, we prove that training a simple decision tree with engineered features can actually achieve high performance even on the independence datasets. In other words, we demonstrate that for cameras, the answer to the research question we tackle can be positive. However, the results also raise new research questions. To apply general machine learning algorithms, and reduce the dependence on manually defined features, we argue the need for a general and suitable representation of network data. We draw analogies with natural language processing, but highlight unique challenges that network data presents.

References

1. Hautala, L.: Why it was so easy to hack the cameras that took down the web. In: CNET Security, October (2016)
2. Palmer, D.: 175,000 IoT cameras can be remotely hacked thanks to flaw, says security researcher. In: ZDNet, July (2017)
3. Yu, T., Sekar, V., Seshan, S., Agarwal, Y., Xu, C.: Handling a trillion (unfixable) flaws on a billion devices: rethinking network security for the internet-of-things. In: Proceedings of the 14th ACM Workshop on Hot Topics in Networks, HotNets-XIV (2015)
4. Sivanathan, A., et al.: Characterizing and classifying IoT traffic in smart cities and campuses. In: IEEE Infocom Workshop Smart Cities and Urban Computing (2017)

5. Miettinen, M., Marchal, S., Hafeez, I., Asokan, N., Sadeghi, A.R., Tarkoma, S.: Iot sentinel demo: automated device-type identification for security enforcement in iot. In: IEEE ICDCS (2017)
6. Meidan, Y., et al.: Profiliot: a machine learning approach for IoT device identification based on network traffic analysis (2017)
7. Guo, H., Heidemann, J.: Ip-based IoT device detection. In: Proceedings of the 2018 Workshop on IoT Security and Privacy, IoT S&P 2018, (New York, NY, USA), pp. 36–42. Association for Computing Machinery (2018)
8. Ortiz, J., Crawford, C., Le, F.: Devicemien: network device behavior modeling for identifying unknown IoT devices. In: Proceedings of the International Conference on Internet of Things Design and Implementation, IoTDI 2019, (New York, NY, USA), pp. 106–117. Association for Computing Machinery (2019)
9. Bremler-Barr, A., Levy, H., Yakhini, Z.: Iot or not: Identifying IoT devices in a shorttime scale (2019)
10. Mazhar, M.H., Shafiq, Z.: Characterizing smart home IoT traffic in the wild (2020)
11. Huang, D.Y., Apthorpe, N., Li, F., Acar, G., Feamster, N.: Iot inspector: crowdsourcing labeled network traffic from smart home devices at scale (2019)
12. Devlin, J., Chang, M.W., Lee, K., Toutanova, K.: BERT: pre-training of deep bidirectional transformers for language understanding. CoRR, vol. abs/1810.04805 (2018)
13. Lan, Z., Chen, M., Goodman, S., Gimpel, K., Sharma, P., Soricut, R.: ALBERT: a lite BERT for self-supervised learning of language representations. CoRR, vol. abs/1909.11942 (2019)
14. Sanh, V., Debut, L., Chaumond, J., Wolf, T.: Distilbert, a distilled version of BERT: smaller, faster, cheaper and lighter. CoRR, vol. abs/1910.01108 (2019)
15. Chen, T., Guestrin, C.: Xgboost: a scalable tree boosting system. CoRR, vol. abs/1603.02754 (2016)
16. Dorogush, A.V., Ershov, V., Gulin, A.: Catboost: gradient boosting with categorical features support. CoRR, vol. abs/1810.11363 (2018)
17. Ke, G., et al.: Lightgbm: a highly efficient gradient boosting decision tree. In: Proceedings of the 31st International Conference on Neural Information Processing Systems, NIPS 2017, (Red Hook, NY, USA), pp. 3149–3157. Curran Associates Inc. (2017)
18. Paxson, V.: Bro: a system for detecting network intruders in real-time. Comput. Netw. **31**(23–24), 2435–2463 (1999)
19. XGBoost eXtreme Gradient Boosting: Machine Learning Challenge Winning Solutions GitHub repository. https://github.com/dmlc/xgboost/tree/master/demo#machine-learning-challenge-winning-solutions. Accessed 21 Mar 2021
20. Light Gradient Boosting Machine: Machine Learning Challenge Winning Solutions GitHub repository. https://github.com/microsoft/LightGBM/blob/master/examples/README.md#machine-learning-challenge-winning-solutions. Accessed 21 Mar 2021
21. Le, F., Srivatsa, M., Verma, D.: Unearthing and exploiting latent semantics behind DNS domains for deep network traffic analysis. In: IJCAI Workshop AI for Internet of Things (2019)
22. Nist internet time servers. https://tf.nist.gov/tf-cgi/servers.cgi
23. B4545 secure view camera ultra-quiet wi-fi garage door opener. https://www.chamberlain.com/secure-view-camera-ultra-quiet-wi-fi-garage-door-opener/p/B4545

IoT Applications in Universities: A Systematic Mapping

Hélio Cardoso de Moura Filho[1]([⊠]), Rubens de Souza Matos Júnior[2],
and Admilson de Ribamar Lima Ribeiro[1]

[1] Federal University of Sergipe, São Cristóvão, Brazil
{helio.cardoso,admilson}@ufs.br
[2] Federal Institute of Sergipe, Lagarto, Brazil
rubens.junior@ifs.edu.br

Abstract. The Internet of Things provides users with a variety of services that enable and intelligent and automated living environment design. University campuses represent an invaluable opportunity to optimize this approach, and smart campus services are already functional in many universities. This article carried out a systematic mapping of the Internet of Things (IoT) scenario within universities. This mapping was guided by research questions which aimed at assessing application areas, technologies, architectures, benefits and drawbacks described throughout the literature. This study selected 451 articles from January 2015 to May 2020 of which 39 articles were used in this systematic mapping. This article noted that resource management has been the main application area of smart campus IoT developments, primarily with a focus on energy issues. Architectures and models to improve data collection, processing, and communication are predominant in the papers we have found. In addition to contributing to researchers in the field, this article will bring a comprehensive view of the Internet of Things (IoT) within universities.

Keywords: Internet of Things · IoT · Smart university · Smart campus

1 Introduction

The Internet of Things (IoT) promotes the effective integration of the real world and the digital world, allowing everyday objects to be connected anywhere at any time, to interact with each other and exchange data and knowledge [6]. IoT provides users with a variety of intelligent services such as environment monitoring and personal detection technologies. It collects information through radio frequency identification, NFC (near field communication), ZigBee, and other wireless and wired networks, and establishes an Internet environment, from the three levels "sensing, networking, and application" to promote an intelligent and automated living environment design [9].

© Springer Nature Switzerland AG 2022
B. Tekinerdogan et al. (Eds.): ICIOT 2021, LNCS 12993, pp. 29–44, 2022.
https://doi.org/10.1007/978-3-030-96068-1_3

According to Fortes et al. [14] university campuses represent an invaluable opportunity to optimize this approach, as they concentrate a large community of students, teachers and staff, forming a "population" that is willing to adopt and promote innovations. In addition, smart campus is already an indispensable part of campus management. Many colleges and universities are now using smart campuses [17].

IoT technology is used to build smart campuses, which can change the interactive mode between multiple organizations and individuals on campus, improve the efficiency of information transmission, make the response more flexible, and create an intelligent campus information service system [40].

Given the growth of applications with IoT technology and the importance of large university centers in adopting them, a systematic mapping was made that in addition to contributing to researchers in the area, will bring a comprehensive view of the Internet of Things (IoT) within universities starting from the initial question: How has the Internet of Things been used within universities?

Smart parking, voice control, energy resource monitoring and control, smart guidance and service, smart rooms and smart student dormitory are just a few of the applications within universities around the world cited in this article.

Therefore, in this article we discuss in the Sect. 2 the research methodology used to perform systematic mapping beyond research questions, search strategies and selections of sources and also inclusion and exclusion criteria. In the Sect. 3 we put the protocol into practice. In the Sect. 4 we show the analysis of the results. And finally in the Sect. 5 we present the conclusion and future work.

2   Research Methodology

The research method of this work was based on the methodology defined by Kitchenham and Charters [23] following the process involving three main phases: Review Planning, Conducting Review and Publication of Results.

With this, this section was subdivided into four parts with activities defined in the planning phase of the review: definition of the objective, research questions, strategies for searching and selecting sources, and inclusion and exclusion criteria.

2.1   Goal Setting

The objective of this systematic mapping is to have a comprehensive view of how the Internet of Things (IoT) has been applied in universities, in addition to contributing to researchers in the area gathering articles that can contribute to the application of IoT in universities and proposition of solutions to problems still open.

2.2   Research Questions

Given the objective set out in the previous section, we defined the following search questions: **QP1.** Which universities use the Internet of Things? **QP2.**

Which applications within universities use the Internet of Things? **QP3.** What technologies are used to use the Internet of Things within universities? **QP4.** What advantages and disadvantages of technologies used in universities when using the Internet of Things? **QP5.** What system architectures have been proposed or used in IoT work in universities?

2.3 Source Research and Selection Strategies

To answer the research questions of the previous topic, we defined five research sources indicated by researchers and experienced professionals in the field as follows: SpringerLink; ScienceDirect; IEEE Xplore; ACM Digital Library; and Google Scholar.

We also define the following search criteria: selecting the articles of the last five years (2015–2020); articles must be written in English or Portuguese; and the article be opened or have full access to the article through the CAPES periodic portal accessible at the Federal University of Sergipe (UFS).

2.4 Inclusion and Exclusion Criteria

Some inclusion and exclusion criteria were defined to select only the articles mention about the Internet of Things in universities. With this, the title of the article should mention internet of things and university, university campus or smart campus and the abstract should also mention internet of things and university, university campus or smart campus. To answer the research questions defined in subsection *Search Questions*, the selected articles must present the internet of things applications in universities, as well as technologies used in these applications and the architectures of systems that were proposed or used in IoT works.

As exclusion criteria it was defined that will be excluded works that are not written in English or Portuguese, as well as works that are not fully available in the databases or that did not meet any inclusion criteria, as well as duplicate articles.

3 Protocol Execution

Given the above in the Sect. 2, in order to obtain the proper answers to the research questions, the first step performed was to execute a search string in all search sources mentioned in the Sect. 2.3. The following search string was used:

("internet of things" OR "IoT") AND ("smart place" OR "smart space" OR "smart environment" OR "smart campus" OR "smart university")

Figure 1 shows the amount of articles returned in the search and their search sources.

You can see in Fig. 2 a year-after-year growth of the internet of things in universities.

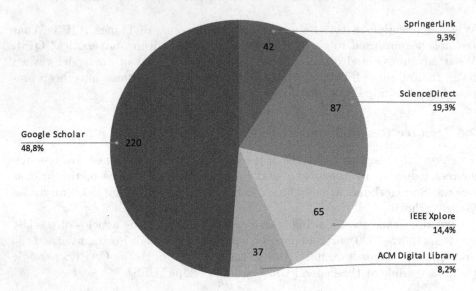

Fig. 1. Number of articles returned in the search and their respective search source

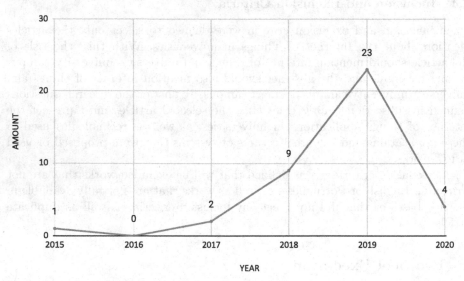

Fig. 2. Number of articles published per year

A first analysis was made observing only the title and abstract and taking into account the inclusion and exclusion criteria previously known. In this analysis, 350 articles were excluded because they did not meet the inclusion and exclusion criteria and 9 articles were excluded by duplicity. Remained 92 articles to be read in full. After the full reading of the 92 articles selected in the previous stage, 53 more articles were excluded because they did not meet the inclusion and exclusion criteria. With this, they totaled 39 articles to extract the answers to the research questions established in the Sect. 2.

4 Results

In this section is presented the result of the analysis of the 39 articles used relating them to the research questions of this article presented in the Sect. 2.

4.1 Which Universities Use the Internet of Things?

Table 1 lists universities whose smart campus applications have been found in literature. Figure 3 demonstrates the location of those universities. Colors represent the amount of articles published. Plot map using highcharter library [24].

Fig. 3. Map of universities using the Internet of Things (IoT)

The articles [2,5,11,21,36,37] could not extract the answer to this research question, so we contacted the authors but got no return. Articles [2,9,13,17,19, 25,30,33,39–42] did not explicitly inform which university the application was applied to or proposed. In these articles, the name of the authors' institution was used when all were from the same institution.

4.2 What Applications Within Universities that Use the Internet of Things?

Each paragraph below mentions not only the applications, but also their proposals defined by the authors.

Smart Parking: In [3] the development of a management platform for charging electric vehicles on a university campus is presented.

Table 1. List of universities using the Internet of Things (IoT)

University	Article
Chonbuk National University, South Korea	[3]
Coimbatore Institute of Technology, Coimbatore	[32]
Federal University of Rio Grande do Norte, Brazil	[31]
Feng Chia University, Taichung, Taiwan	[10]
Fifth People's Hospital of Qinghai Province, Xining, P.R. China	[25]
Harrisburg University of Science and Technology, Harrisburg, Pennsylvania, USA	[1]
Hebei University of Technology, Tianjin, China	[39]
Institut Teknologi Sumatera, Lampung Selatan, Indonesia	[41,42]
Lancaster University, England	[7]
Nanjing University of Posts and Telecommunications (NUPT), China	[18]
National Chiao Tung University (NCTU), Hsinchu, Taiwan	[26,27]
National Taitung University, Taitung, Taiwan	[9]
North China University of Science and Technology, Tangshan, China	[13,40]
Rhodes University, South Africa	[33]
Tampere University of Technology, Finland	[29]
Tokyo Denki University, Japan	[28]
Toyo University, Japan	[22]
University of A Coruña (UDC), Spain	[16]
University of Brescia, Brescia, Italy	[8,34,35]
University of Calabria, Italy	[15]
University of California, USA	[38]
University of Information Technology VNU-HCM, Vietnam	[30]
University of New South Wales Sydney, Sydney, Australia	[33]
University of Oulu, Oulu, Finland	[20]
University of Parma, Italy	[12]
University of Rajshahi, Bangladesh	[19]
Xinxiang University, Xinxiang, China	[17]
Yildiz Technical University, Istanbul, Turkey	[4]

Smart Voice Control: In [32] an implementation is presented whose purpose is to control and monitor items such as lights, fans, projector and lab air conditioning using the Google assistant or chat robot.

Monitoring and Control of Energy Resources Distributed Using LoRaWAN: In [31] an IoT architecture capable of transparently managing different communication protocols in smart environments is presented and investigates its possible application for monitoring and control of distributed energy resources on a smart campus.

Orientation and Intelligent Campus Service with Facial Recognition: In [10] is presented an intelligent structure of care and guidance on campus with facial recognition based on deep learning.

Intelligent Medical Data Monitoring System: In [25] medical data monitoring is presented that includes physiological data collection, data processing, and real-time data transmission.

Smart Classroom: In [1] a smart classroom environment is presented to provide students and teachers with a better learning and teaching environment.

Teaching Performance Evaluation System: In [39] is presented the construction of a big data network teaching platform, based on education and big data teaching, combined with principal component analysis and AHP to determine the performance evaluation system, and use the gray correlation grade to improve the TOPSIS method to establish the teacher network teaching performance evaluation model.

Power Monitoring System: In [41] the development of a prototype energy monitoring system for buildings is presented.

Smart Rooms: In [42] the implementation of smart room technology to increase energy efficiency is presented.

Power Information System: In [7] the data integration of existing power management systems and buildings is presented to enable integrated analysis and optimization.

Security System: In [2] a security framework is presented that would improve security on a university campus in order to strengthen campus security and reduce costs.

Intelligent Service System: In [18] an intelligent service system architecture (SSS) is presented.

CampusTalk: In [26] CampusTalk is presented that provides convenient access to cyber and physical devices through web technology. CampusTalk's main app is SmartPhoneTalk, which allows other apps to be accessed by students through their smartphones without installing mobile apps.

DormTalk - Smart Student Dormitory: In [27], the authors present how edge computing and cloud computing can be well integrated to create a smart environment.

Decentralized Smart Network System Based on Campus Street Lights: In [9] is presented an edge computing network on campus in the process of co-designing hardware and software. The system employs street lighting as the

IoT network communication node device. A transmission network of edge computing nodes to provide IoT information processing, temporary storage, and transmission.

Smart Bus System: In [13] a proposal is presented to improve the quality and efficiency of bus service to meet the travel needs of citizens.

Situational Awareness System on Smart Campus: In [40] a proposal is presented that provides services to teachers and students through a powerful perceptual database.

Intelligent Transport System: In [33] is presented the bike sharing platform.

Developing Smart Services: In [29] a proposal is presented to clarify how smart facility services can be developed in the context of smart campus.

Protocol for Video Collection and Vital Data: In [28] a protocol for collecting data from the behavior of teachers and students in different class types using video and wearable device is presented.

Smartwatch App to Help Students with disabilities: In [22] a prototype application is presented that helps students with disabilities perform daily life tasks within a building.

3D-Launching Radio Planning Simulator: In [16] the use of a LoRaWAN fog computing-based architecture is presented to provide connectivity to IoT nodes deployed on a campus.

Energy Management and Comfort of Educational Spaces: In [34] the monitoring of internal conditions in educational spaces and to predict strategies and scenarios related to the energy demand defined by the flow of occupation.

Artificial Neural Network for Prediction and Performance of Ventilation Patterns: In [35] a proposal is presented to define patterns of opening or closing of automated windows to improve indoor air quality in educational spaces.

Internal and External Location Services for LoRaWAN: In [8] a proposal is presented use of LPWANs with location techniques for Smart Campus applications.

Smart UniCal - Agent-Oriented Cooperative Smart Objects: In [15] a proposal is presented to explore an agent-based computing paradigm to support the analysis, design, and implementation of IoT systems.

Enhanced VIRE Location Algorithm in the Context of the 5G Network: In [38] a proposal is presented to provide guidance for the 5G network to be applied in smart campus construction.

An IoT Reconfiguration Framework - Ontology-Based Modeling and Bayesian Reasoning for Context Management: In [30] a reconfiguration structure of IoTs after changes in complex contexts.

Classroom Occupancy Monitoring System: In [30] classroom underutilization and optimal classroom allocation are presented.

Architecture and Operational Model for Digital Infrastructure: In [20] a technical architecture for the future Smart Campus is presented, consisting of 5G and IoT networks, complemented by distributed computing and data analysis.

Wearable App: In [12] a wearable application is presented for interacting with smart objects.

Phone Call Server: In [21] a deployment of the phone call change server integrated into a SIP-based private network is presented.

Intelligent Environment Monitoring, Smart Parking and Smart Canteen: In [19] a smart campus model is presented to achieve intelligent management and service on campus.

Digital Warning Frame Platform: In [11] an interactive message exchange architecture based on the MQTT (Message Queuing Telemetry Transport) protocol is presented that deeply engages users in the IoT process.

PLC Automatic Ticketing System: In [17] a system that includes the design and application of subsystems such as consumption, library management and presence management system is presented.

ZigBee and LoRa-Based Communication System: In [4] is presented a diversified communication system with intelligent features.

Disaster Management System: In [5] a new Named Data Network Disaster Management (NDN-DM) disaster management system.

Sustainable Smart Campus: In [37]a proposal for data acquisition through IoT, data centralization in a proprietary infrastructure and data management and analysis using big data is presented.

Application of a Big Data Framework for Data Monitoring: In [36] a big data framework capable of analyzing the data is presented, regardless of its format, providing effective and efficient responses to each process.

The above data were grouped according to the type of application. It is important to highlight that articles can be categorized into more than one group, so Fig. 4 shows the categorized data.

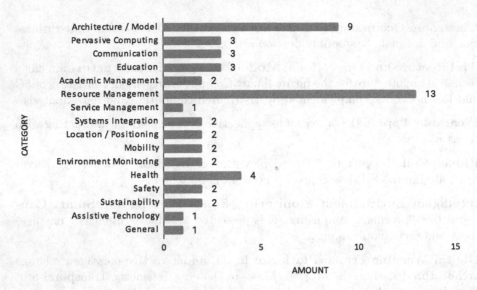

Fig. 4. Category of articles as to the type of application

4.3 What Technologies Are Used to Use the Internet of Things Within Universities?

To answer this research question, we subdivided into three sub-items: sensors or actuators; processing and; communication.

Sensors or Actuators. As seen in the previous sections, a diversity of applications were proposed by several authors. With this, the most diverse types of sensors and actuators were used to capture the data of the environment. It was also observed that the temperature sensor was the most used sensor among the authors. With this sensor, for example, in Tagliabue et al. [34] presented the monitoring of internal conditions to unveil critical situations defined by temperature, humidity and indoor air quality in educational spaces and to predict strategies and scenarios related to the energy demand defined by the flow of occupation.

Accelerometers, Beam counter, RFID, Sensor Light Dependent Resistor (LDR), CO and CO2 sensor, Sensor PM2.5 (air quality), Electric current sensor, Electricity monitoring sensor, Solar radiation sensor, Temperature sensor, Humidity sensor, Presence sensor (PIR), iBeacon and other various types of sensors have been used by the authors.

Processing. Arduino, Edge computing devices, Microprocessors and microcontrollers, Raspberry Pi, Central/local server are the processing technologies used in mapped articles.

Communication. The communication technologies used by the authors in the mapped articles are: ADSL, Bluetooth, LoRaWAN, Fiber optics, GSM, GPRS, EDGE, WCDMA, CDMA2000 1X e EV-DO, TD-SCDMA, LTE, Narrowband-IoT (NB-IoT) - LPWAN, NFC (Near Field Communication), RFID, 4G/5G Network, Ultra Wide Band Network (UWB), Wired network, Wireless Sensor Network (WSN), Radio IEEE 802.15.4, WiFi and Zigbee.

4.4 What Advantages and Disadvantages of Technologies Used in Universities When Using the Internet of Things?

Most articles speak of the advantages, be it the advantages of the application or even the advantages of using a certain type of sensor/actuator, processing or communication. However, not all articles mention the disadvantages.

In [31], its main disadvantage that LoRaWAN technology is represented by limited data throughput. Key features are flexibility, scalability, wide diffusion and availability of modules from many manufacturers.

In [7], provide strategic supervision helping reduce the energy waste of over-heated buildings, however the data tells a story about energy consumption, but not the reason or how it is being consumed.

In [33], reports that classroom occupancy monitoring system is relatively low cost, easy deployment, high accuracy and good privacy protection. However the beam counter can count more than one individual as just one when they pass side by side.

Figure 5 then shows the categorized benefits data. It is important to emphasize that articles can be classified into more than one group.

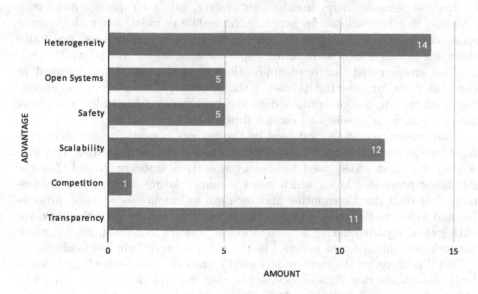

Fig. 5. Category of articles for benefits

4.5 What System Architectures Have Been Proposed or Used in IoT Work in Universities?

The selected articles considered several architectures as 3 layers, 4 layers, 5 layers, 6 layers, Cluster, Edge computing, Cloud computing and NDN (Named Data Network).

The predominant architecture was the three-layer architecture (usually, sensor layer, communication layer and application layer). The sensor layer is where the devices used to acquire physical information and convert it into a form suitable for processing meet. The communication layer collects data from sensors and aggregates the output through Wi-Fi networks, LANs. The application layer, the information is brought back to the physical world in a processed and precisely analyzed form.

5   Conclusion

This work performed a systematic mapping in research sources relevant to the area of computer science following predefined inclusion and exclusion criteria. This selection resulted in the analysis and extraction of 39 articles relevant to the research questions. This work besides contributing to researchers in the area on the main types of applications, sensor and actuator technologies, processing technologies, communication technologies, advantages and disadvantages, and also the architectures used in the use of internet of things (IoT) within universities, also aims to guide future research related to the Internet of Things in universities.

Improvements in energy management, safety, indoor air quality, room temperature, mobility, facilities for people with disabilities to interact with the environment, classroom management, among many other applications, make this there is a growth of internet of things applications in universities year after year.

This article noted that most applications treated resource management as the main point for using the internet of things primarily with a focus on energy. Secondly, the applications proposed an architecture/model in order to improve data collection, processing and communication.

The sensors/actuators most used by the authors in capturing the data were temperature sensors, humidity sensors and video cameras. Regarding data processing, the most widely used technology was the Raspberry Pi and then the intelligent processing layer, which was the nomenclature used to describe systems that used cloud computing and big data techniques for storage, processing and access to the collected data. Regarding communication technology, the authors who reported having used the wireless network without specifying which network, was inferred that it would be the Wi-fi network (wireless fidelity).

Wi-fi is therefore the most widely used communication technology followed by Bluetooth and then Zigbee. Most applications have made use of the principles of heterogeneity and scalability drawn in a 3 (three) layer-based architecture.

For future work it is suggested to conduct studies to evaluate the use of the Internet of things in teaching hospitals (university hospitals) as a way to improve the learning of students from various areas such as medicine, physiotherapy, nursing and etc., besides contributing to the improvement of the process benefiting mainly users/patients who make use of the network.

References

1. Abdellatif, I.: Towards a novel approach for designing smart classrooms. In: 2019 IEEE 2nd International Conference on Information and Computer Technologies, ICICT 2019, pp. 280–284 (2019). https://doi.org/10.1109/INFOCT.2019.8711355
2. Abdullah, A., Thanoon, M., Alsulami, A.: Toward a smart campus using IoT: framework for safety and security system on a university campus. Adv. Sci. Technol. Eng. Syst. **4**(5), 97–103 (2019). https://doi.org/10.25046/aj040512
3. Ahmed, M.A., Alsayyari, A.S., Kim, Y.C.: System architecture based on IoT for smart campus parking lots. In: 2nd International Conference on Computer Applications and Information Security, ICCAIS 2019, pp. 1–4 (2019). https://doi.org/10.1109/CAIS.2019.8769477
4. Ali, A.I., Partal, S.Z., Kepke, S., Partal, H.P.: ZigBee and LoRa based wireless sensors for smart environment and IoT applications. In: Proceedings - 2019 IEEE 1st Global Power, Energy and Communication Conference, GPECOM 2019, pp. 19–23 (2019). https://doi.org/10.1109/GPECOM.2019.8778505
5. Ali, Z., Shah, M.A., Almogren, A., Ud Din, I., Maple, C., Khattak, H.A.: Named data networking for efficient IoT-based disaster management in a smart campus. Sustainability **12**(8), 3088 (2020). https://doi.org/10.3390/su12083088. https://www.mdpi.com/2071-1050/12/8/3088
6. Amadeo, M., Ruggeri, G., Campolo, C., Molinaro, A., Loscrí, V., Calafate, C.T.: Fog computing in IoT smart environments via named data networking: a study on service orchestration mechanisms. Future Internet **11**(11), 222 (2019). https://doi.org/10.3390/fi11110222. https://www.mdpi.com/1999-5903/11/11/222
7. Bates, O., Friday, A.: Beyond data in the smart city: repurposing existing campus IoT. IEEE Pervasive Comput. **16**(2), 54–60 (2017). https://doi.org/10.1109/MPRV.2017.30
8. Bonafini, F., et al.: Evaluating indoor and outdoor localization services for LoRaWAN in Smart City applications. In: 2019 IEEE International Workshop on Metrology for Industry 4.0 and IoT, MetroInd 4.0 and IoT 2019 - Proceedings, pp. 300–305 (2019). https://doi.org/10.1109/METROI4.2019.8792901
9. Chang, Y.C., Lai, Y.H.: Campus edge computing network based on IoT street lighting nodes. IEEE Syst. J. **14**(1), 164–171 (2020). https://doi.org/10.1109/JSYST.2018.2873430
10. Chen, L.W., Chen, T.P., Chen, D.E., Liu, J.X., Tsai, M.F.: Smart campus care and guiding with dedicated video footprinting through Internet of Things technologies. IEEE Access **6**, 43956–43966 (2018). https://doi.org/10.1109/ACCESS.2018.2856251
11. Chen, P.W., Chen, Y.H., Wu, Y.H.: Pushing the digital notice board toward ubiquitous based on the concept of the internet of everything. In: Proceedings - 2019 12th International Conference on Ubi-Media Computing, Ubi-Media 2019, pp. 230–235 (2019). https://doi.org/10.1109/Ubi-Media.2019.00052
12. Cirani, S., Picone, M.: Wearable computing for the Internet of Things. IT Prof. **17**(5), 35–41 (2015). https://doi.org/10.1109/MITP.2015.89

13. Feng, X., Zhang, J., Chen, J., Wang, G., Zhang, L., Li, R.: Design of intelligent bus positioning based on Internet of Things for smart campus. IEEE Access **6**, 60005–60015 (2018). https://doi.org/10.1109/ACCESS.2018.2874083

14. Fortes, S., et al.: The campus as a smart city: University of Málaga environmental, learning, and research approaches. Sensors **19**, 1349 (2019). https://doi.org/10.3390/s19061349

15. Fortino, G., Russo, W., Savaglio, C., Shen, W., Zhou, M.: Agent-oriented cooperative smart objects: from IoT system design to implementation. IEEE Trans. Syst. Man Cybern. Syst. **48**(11), 1949–1956 (2018). https://doi.org/10.1109/TSMC.2017.2780618

16. Fraga-Lamas, P., et al.: Design and experimental validation of a LoRaWAN fog computing based architecture for IoT enabled smart campus applications. Sensors **19**(15), 3287 (2019). https://doi.org/10.3390/s19153287

17. Guo, G.: Design and implementation of smart campus automatic settlement PLC control system for Internet of Things. IEEE Access **6**, 62601–62611 (2018). https://doi.org/10.1109/ACCESS.2018.2877023

18. Guo, Y., Zhu, H., Yang, L.: Smart service system (SSS): a novel architecture enabling coordination of heterogeneous networking technologies and devices for Internet of Things. China Commun. **14**(3), 130–144 (2017). https://doi.org/10.1109/CC.2017.7897329

19. Hossain, I., Das, D., Rashed, M.G.: Internet of Things based model for smart campus: challenges and limitations. In: 5th International Conference on Computer, Communication, Chemical, Materials and Electronic Engineering, IC4ME2 2019, pp. 11–12 (2019). https://doi.org/10.1109/IC4ME247184.2019.9036629

20. Jurva, R., Matinmikko-Blue, M., Niemelä, V., Nenonen, S.: Architecture and operational model for smart campus digital infrastructure. Wirel. Pers. Commun. **113**(3), 1437–1454 (2020). https://doi.org/10.1007/s11277-020-07221-5

21. Karbari, S., Dhanne, B.: Practical design and implementation of smart campus on IoT platform. Ijaema. Com **XI**, 3857–3864 (2019). http://www.ijaema.com/gallery/449-september-2516.pdf

22. Kim, J.E., Bessho, M., Sakamura, K.: Towards a smartwatch application to assist students with disabilities in an IoT-enabled campus. In: 2019 IEEE 1st Global Conference on Life Sciences and Technologies, LifeTech 2019 (LifeTech), pp. 243–246 (2019). https://doi.org/10.1109/LifeTech.2019.8883995

23. Kitchenham, B., Charters, S.: Guidelines for performing systematic literature reviews in software engineering (2007)

24. Kunst, J.: Highcharter: A Wrapper for the 'Highcharts' Library (2020). R package version 0.8.2. https://CRAN.R-project.org/package=highcharter

25. Liang, Y., Chen, Z.: Intelligent and real-time data acquisition for medical monitoring in smart campus. IEEE Access **6**, 74836–74846 (2018). https://doi.org/10.1109/ACCESS.2018.2883106

26. Lin, Y.B., Chen, L.K., Shieh, M.Z., Lin, Y.W., Yen, T.H.: CampusTalk: IoT devices and their interesting features on campus applications. IEEE Access **6**, 26036–26046 (2018). https://doi.org/10.1109/ACCESS.2018.2832222

27. Lin, Y.B., Shieh, M.Z., Lin, Y.W.: DormTalk: edge computing for the dormitory applications on campus. IET Netw. **8**(3), 179–188 (2019). https://doi.org/10.1049/iet-net.2018.5178

28. Matsui, K., Kasai, T., Sakai, K.: Challenges for data collecting of teacher and student' behavior in different types of class using video and wearable device. In: 2019 Joint 8th International Conference on Informatics, Electronics and Vision, ICIEV 2019 and 3rd International Conference on Imaging, Vision and Pattern Recognition, icIVPR 2019 with International Conference on Activity and Behavior Computing, ABC 2019, pp. 56–61 (2019). https://doi.org/10.1109/ICIEV.2019.8858558

29. Nenonen, S., van Wezel, R., Niemi, O.: Developing Smart Services to Smart Campus, pp. 289–295. Emerald Publishing Limited, May 2019. https://doi.org/10.1108/s2516-285320190000002006

30. Nguyen-Anh, T., Le-Trung, Q.: An IoT reconfiguration framework applied ontology-based modeling and Bayesian-based reasoning for context management. In: Proceedings - 2019 6th NAFOSTED Conference on Information and Computer Science, NICS 2019, pp. 540–545 (2019). https://doi.org/10.1109/NICS48868.2019.9023885

31. Pasetti, M., Ferrari, P., Silva, D.R.C., Silva, I., Sisinni, E.: On the use of LoRaWAN for the monitoring and control of distributed energy resources in a smart campus. Appl. Sci. **10**(1), 320 (2020). https://doi.org/10.3390/app10010320. https://www.mdpi.com/2076-3417/10/1/320

32. Poongothai, M., Sundar, K., Vinayak, B.: Implementation of IoT based intelligent voice controlled laboratory using Google assistant. Int. J. Comput. Appl. **182**(16), 6–10 (2018). https://doi.org/10.5120/ijca2018917808

33. Sutjarittham, T., Gharakheili, H.H., Kanhere, S.S., Sivaraman, V.: Experiences with IoT and AI in a smart campus for optimizing classroom usage. IEEE Internet Things J. **6**, 7595–7607 (2019). https://doi.org/10.1109/JIOT.2019.2902410

34. Tagliabue, L.C., Cecconi, F.R., Rinaldi, S., Flammini, A., Ciribini, A.L.: Energy and comfort management of the educational spaces through IoT network for IAQ assessment in the eLUX lab. In: IOP Conference Series: Earth and Environmental Science, vol. 296, no. 1 (2019). https://doi.org/10.1088/1755-1315/296/1/012056

35. Tagliabue, L.C., Re Cecconi, F., Rinadi, S., Ciribini, A.L.: IoT network-based ANN for ventilation pattern prediction and actuation to optimize IAQ in educational spaces. In: IOP Conference Series: Materials Science and Engineering, vol. 609, no. 4 (2019). https://doi.org/10.1088/1757-899X/609/4/042042

36. Villegas-Ch, W., Molina-Enriquez, J., Chicaiza-Tamayo, C., Ortiz-Garcés, I., Luján-Mora, S.: Application of a big data framework for data monitoring on a smart campus. Sustainability **11**(20), 5552 (2019). https://doi.org/10.3390/su11205552. https://www.mdpi.com/2071-1050/11/20/5552

37. Villegas-Ch, W., Palacios-Pacheco, X., Luján-Mora, S.: Application of a smart city model to a traditional university campus with a big data architecture: a sustainable smart campus. Sustainability **11**(10), 2857 (2019). https://doi.org/10.3390/su11102857. https://www.mdpi.com/2071-1050/11/10/2857

38. Xu, X., et al.: Research on key technologies of smart campus teaching platform based on 5G network. IEEE Access **7**, 20664–20675 (2019). https://doi.org/10.1109/ACCESS.2019.2894129

39. Xu, X., Wang, Y., Yu, S.: Teaching performance evaluation in smart campus. IEEE Access **6**, 77754–77766 (2018). https://doi.org/10.1109/ACCESS.2018.2884022

40. Yang, A.M., Li, S.S., Ren, C.H., Liu, H.X., Han, Y., Liu, L.: Situational awareness system in the smart campus. IEEE Access **6**, 63976–63986 (2018). https://doi.org/10.1109/ACCESS.2018.2877428

41. Yuliansyah, H., Corio, D., Yunmar, R.A., Aziz, M.R.: Energy monitoring system based on Internet of Things toward smart campus in Institut Teknologi Sumatera. In: IOP Conference Series: Earth and Environmental Science, vol. 258, no. 1 (2019). https://doi.org/10.1088/1755-1315/258/1/012008
42. Yuliansyah, H., Corio, D., Yunmar, R.A., Kahar Aziz, M.R.: Smart-room technology implementation based on Internet of Things toward smart campus in Institut Teknologi Sumatera. In: IOP Conference Series: Earth and Environmental Science, vol. 258, no. 1 (2019). https://doi.org/10.1088/1755-1315/258/1/012053

Middleware of Enterprise 5G Messaging Services: Design and Implementation

Han Wang[1,2,3,4]([envelope]), Bingjiang Peng[3,4], Chunxiao Xing[1,2], and Liang-Jie Zhang[3,4]

[1] Research Institute of Information Technology, Beijing National Research Center for Information Science and Technology, Tsinghua University, Beijing 100084, China
[2] Department of Computer Science and Technology, Institute of Internet Industry, Tsinghua University, Beijing 100084, China
[3] National Engineering Research Center for Supporting Software of Enterprise Internet Services, Shenzhen 518057, China
[4] Kingdee Research, Kingdee International Software Group Company Limited, Shenzhen 518057, China

Abstract. From the aged 2G era to now, short message is consistently playing an important role in both personal and commercial use. Along with the evolution of cellular systems, Rich Communication Services (RCS), which can provide rich-media messages and diverse interactions, has been proposed as an update of the obsolete text-based Short Message Services (SMS) to meet various requirements of modern applications. In China, the three major mobile network operators have jointly launched "5G Messaging Services (5GMS)", a brand new RCS-based telecommunication business in the 5G era, to bring new user experience to individuals and valuable commercial opportunities to enterprises. Currently, most of the enterprise-level applications are delivered in the form of Software-as-a-Service (SaaS), and 5GMS can be utilized as a new entrance for various SaaS applications ideally thanks to its inherent advantages of nativeness, lightweight, interactivity, and security. In this paper, we design a 5GMS-to-SaaS middleware, which can deal with practical issues such as message transmission, format conversion, and account matching, to facilitate establishing connections between the unified front-end 5GMS and a large amount of various back-end SaaS applications. The proposed middleware can normalize and simplify the procedures of linking massive services, so as to promote development efficiency and accelerate business extension of various enterprise-level 5GMS-based SaaS applications.

Keywords: 5G Messaging Services · Middleware · Enterprise applications

1 Introduction

The Short Message Services (SMS) [1], originally defined for the Global System for Mobile Communications (GSM) in 1986, facilitates communicating with

This work is supported by National Key R&D Program of China (2018YFB1404401).

B. Tekinerdogan et al. (Eds.): ICIOT 2021, LNCS 12993, pp. 45–57, 2022.
https://doi.org/10.1007/978-3-030-96068-1_4

individuals or commercial services by exchanging plain text messages, and thus rapidly becomes the most popular business since the beginning of the 2G era. With the rapid spread of 3G/4G mobile networks and smart terminals, the traditional SMS become increasingly unable to meet diverse requirements due to its inherent text-only limitation. Hence in 2008, the GSM Association (GSMA) introduces the new Rich Communication Services (RCS) [2] to update the obsolete SMS. The RCS can provide rich-media messages and diverse interactions, and also the specifications [3–7] are evolving constantly from the initial "Release 1" to the latest "Universal Profile Version 2.4 (UP 2.4)" to support various new requirements of the users.

In 2020, the beginning year of 5G era in China, a brand-new telecommunication business "5G Messaging Services (5GMS)" [8], based on the latest GSMA RCS UP 2.4 specifications [7], has been launched jointly by the three major Mobile Network Operators (MNOs). The 5GMS system is deployed on the IP Multimedia Subsystem (IMS) of the MNO's 5G core network, while the 5GMS application is embedded as a native system-level essential function in smart terminals providing enhanced user interface and service experience with richer contents including text, audio, video, image, location and etc. The 5GMS brings not only rich-media messages and diverse interactions, but also a most important service paradigm of "Messaging as a Platform (MaaP) + Chatbot Services Provider (CSP)". Based on MaaP and CSP, enterprises can build chatbots to provide online business services to their customers, while the customers can simply search a specific chatbot in their smart terminals at any time, and then have conversation with interactive rich-media messages and cards to access the provided services. With 5GMS, the users conveniently obtain personalized service from enterprises, and the enterprises also have a new and valuable channel for providing intelligent services and getting user feedback, and hence having closer connection with their customers. Therefore, the "Enterprise 5GMS" is so attractive that can bring new user experience to individuals and valuable commercial opportunities to enterprises [9].

Nowadays, with the widespread adoption of cloud computing, more and more services are provided in the form of Software-as-a-Service (SaaS) applications, and 5GMS can be utilized as a new entrance for various enterprise-level SaaS applications with the help of CSP. However, most of the CSPs are designed for managing general purpose chatbots, providing only limited functions for linking enterprise-level services. Actually, there are quite a lot of practical issues, such as message transmission, format conversion, and account matching, for establishing connections between the unified front-end 5GMS and a large amount of various back-end SaaS applications. Hence, it is necessary to develop a 5GMS-to-SaaS middleware between CSP and enterprise to normalize and simplify the procedures of linking massive services, so as to promote development efficiency and accelerate business extension of various enterprise-level 5GMS-based SaaS applications.

In this paper, we design and implement a 5GMS-to-SaaS middleware to facilitate establishing connections between front-end and back-end services. The rest of this paper is organized as follows. In Sect. 2, we introduce the architecture of the 5GMS-to-SaaS system, and propose the general function design of the 5GMS middleware. Then, we propose the internal workflow and implement the above core functions of the middleware in Sect. 3. At last, the paper is concluded in Sect. 4.

2 General Design of 5GMS Middleware

Middleware is the key enabling technique to connect the front-end 5GMS with various back-end SaaS applications. In this section, we first introduce the general system architecture of the "5GMS-Middleware-SaaS" paradigm, and then design the function architecture of the 5GMS middleware.

2.1 System Architecture

Generally, a typical 5GMS-to-SaaS System consists of four roles: User, MNO, CSP and Enterprise. The physical and corresponding logical architectures of the system are illustrated in Fig. 1 and Fig. 2 respectively, and discussed in detail as follows.

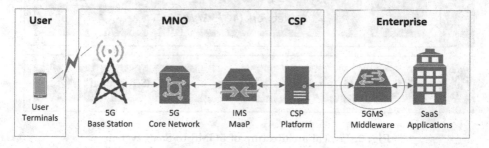

Fig. 1. Physical architecture of 5GMS-to-SaaS system

Use. Users get in touch with the provided Enterprise SaaS though smart terminals. The 5GMS application is a native system-level essential function embedded in smart terminals, providing enhanced user interface and service experience with richer contents including text, audio, video, image, location and etc. If the terminal does not support the specifications of GSMA RCS UP 2.4, the 5GMS message will fallback to plain SMS with brief information and external URL to ensure the compatibility.

MNO. MNOs are responsible for providing the basic network and MaaP capability of the 5GMS system, where the network is not limited to the 5G system and is also capable for IMS-enabled 4G or WiFi systems which has MaaP capabilities. Based on the IMS, MaaP combines the features of advanced messaging

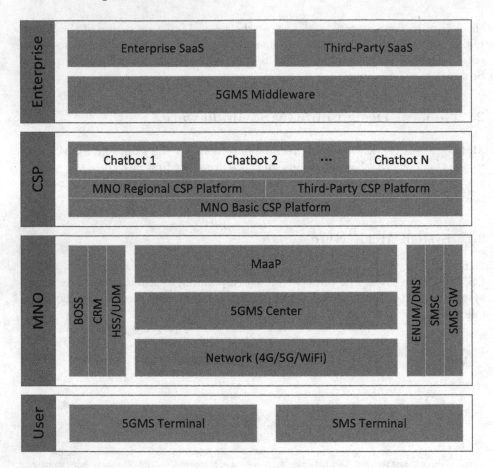

Fig. 2. Logical architecture of 5GMS-to-SaaS system

with standard interfaces to chatbots and plugins, creating a richer experience for consumers and allowing enterprises to realize the potential 5GMS-to-SaaS paradigm of IP messaging.

CSP. CSPs are responsible for and providing chatbot services by connecting MNO's MaaP and Enterprise's businesses. Since the functions of CSP and MaaP are tightly connected with each other, MNOs usually choose to build a nation-wide primary basic CSP platform directly connecting to their core network's MaaP. Then, based on the primary platform, the secondary CSPs can be carried by MNO's regional platform (usually divided by provinces) or third-party's platforms for the purpose of offloading message traffic.

Enterprise. With the help of CSP, enterprise can provide its own businesses through a chatbot. Actually, it is so complicated that both self-operated and third-party SaaS applications should be integrated into a single chatbot to ensure the critical requirements of enterprise businesses. Hence, it is necessary to introduce a "5GMS Middleware" to deal with various complicate problems of integrating massive SaaS applications into a single 5GMS chatbot.

2.2   Function Design

The MNO's nation-wide primary CSP platform is responsible for directly connecting to core network's MaaP, while the secondary CSPs are usually designed for building and managing general purpose chatbots, providing only limited functions for linking enterprise-level services. There are quite a lot of practical issues for establishing connections between the unified front-end 5GMS and a large amount of various back-end SaaS applications. Therefore, we design a 5GMS-to-SaaS middleware in Fig. 3, locating between the secondary CSP and the Enterprise in Fig. 2, to normalize and simplify the procedures of linking massive services so as to promote development efficiency and accelerate business extension of various enterprise-level 5GMS-based SaaS applications.

As illustrated in Fig. 3, our proposed 5GMS middleware mainly consists of three functional modules (Message Transmission, Format Conversion, and Account Matching) and a controlling module (Management Console), whose functions are explained in detail as follows.

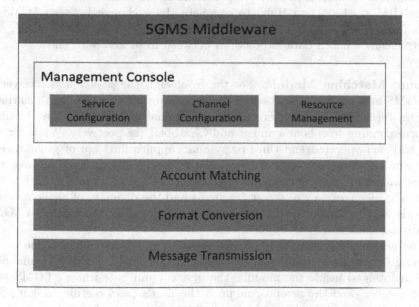

Fig. 3. Function architecture of 5GMS middleware

Message Transmission Module. The fundamental function of the middleware is to transmit 5GMS messages between the chatbot and the SaaS applications, where the former is hosted on the CSP platform, and the latter are provided by the enterprises or third parties and hosted on the cloud platform. The process of message transmission relates not only receiving and sending packages, but also processing their internal contents which should be supported by the modules of Format Conversion and Account Matching collaboratively.

The message transmission module is responsible for receiving, processing, and sending 5GMS message packages, and hence is the core function of the middleware which will be discussed in detail in Sect. 3.

Format Conversion Module. The front-end 5GMS message is described in JSON format following the specifications of GSMA RCS UP 2.4 [7], while due to various practical considerations, the back-end SaaS applications from enterprises and third parties use various formats (e.g., XML, YAML, JSON, CSV, and etc.) to exchange data which brings great trouble to the front-to-back data interaction.

The format conversion module is responsible for converting the various back-end data formats to the front-end JSON format in a uniform manner. The Cloud Information Model (CIM) [10] is an open source data exchange model proposed by the Linux Foundation that provides an open specification based on existing standards for connecting multiple enterprise services to guarantee their interoperability. By calling data converting interfaces, the format conversion module adopts CIM as the "Data Hub" to complete the exchange between 5GMS in JSON format and SaaS in other formats (e.g., XML, YAML, JSON, CSV, and etc.) to ensure smooth data interactions between front and back ends.

Account Matching Module. For the front end, the sender and receiver of the 5GMS message are described by corresponding "from" and "to" identifiers (IDs) in the JSON body, where the user terminal and chatbot are identified by corresponding telephone number and ChatbotID respectively. While for the back end, self-operated and third-party SaaS applications are of great variety and quantity, whose accounts are identified by user name or email address and authenticated by various methods (e.g., Session-Cookie, Token, OAuth2, and SSO). The inconsistency of account systems and the diversity of authentication methods lead to difficulties in connecting and managing the front-end 5GMS and various back-end SaaS applications.

The account matching module is responsible for achieving the one-to-one mapping between the front-end and back-end accounts. There is a mapping table maintained inside the module: the first column is the user's 5GMS telephone number, and the second column is the user's SaaS certificate (e.g., SessionID, Token) which is obtained when first use and auto-refreshed periodically. In this way, the accounts and certificates between front and back ends are connected together by the mapping table, and users can access various SaaS applications through 5GMS terminal without frequent manual login and authentication, which improves user experience significantly.

Management Console Module. Since there are a large number of back-end SaaS applications to connect with the front-end 5GMS, it is necessary to uniformly manage the procedures of message transmission, format conversion and account matching.

The management console module is responsible for uniformly controlling services, channels and resources so as to promote the management efficiency, where its detailed functions are described as follows.

- **Service Configuration** is responsible for registering the back-end SaaS applications, and configuring their critical parameters of transmission modes, data formats, and account systems.
- **Channel Configuration** is responsible for configuring the availability of front-to-end channels for SaaS applications so as to control the user access permissions.
- **Resource Management** is responsible for managing and maintaining the resources inside the 5GMS middleware, such as message templates, media pools, databases, and etc.

With the unified control of the management console, the resources of each module in the 5GMS middleware can be coordinated effectively to ensure efficient, smooth and secure transmission to facilitate the front-to-back ends connections.

3   Implementation Scheme of 5GMS Middleware

The fundamental function of the 5GMS middleware is to transmit messages between the front-end chatbot and the back-end various SaaS applications. In this section, we first propose the general workflow of transmitting messages inside the 5GMS middleware, and then gives the corresponding practical implementation scheme.

3.1   General Workflow

According to Sect. 2.2, the core function of the 5GMS middleware is transmitting and processing message packages, and performing user requests to access back-end SaaS applications, which are supported by its internal functional and controlling modules simultaneously.

For the sake of clarity, the message transmission directions are regulated as: (1) Uplink: from user to enterprise; (2) Downlink: from enterprise to user. The general workflow of the middleware can be summarized as receiving uplink message, analyzing package content, performing access request and sending downlink message, which are illustrated in Fig. 4 and explained in detail as follows.

Receive Uplink Message. In the uplink direction, a user generated message is transmitted to the primary CSP platform through the MNO's network, and then the chatbot hosted on the secondary CSP platform receives and forwards the message package to the 5GMS middleware for further processing.

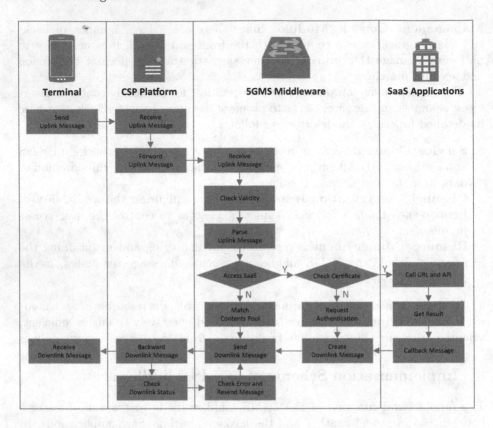

Fig. 4. Message transmission workflow in 5GMS middleware

Analyze Package Content. In the middleware, the received 5GMS message should be analyzed to get the user's requests. After checked the validity, the message package is parsed to get its header and body. If the parsed message body shows that the user request is explicit, the middleware will start the procedure of accessing back-end SaaS applications. Otherwise, the middleware will perform the message matching procedure to determine the user's intentions.

Perform Access Request. When user request is explicit, the middleware will perform the accessing SaaS procedures. By getting authenticated and calling URL/API, the callback result will be assembled into a downlink message.

Send Downlink Message. At last, the created downlink message will be send back from middleware, CSP platform, to the user terminal. In the downlink direction, the CSP platform is responsible for checking the sending status. If the message cannot be returned successfully, the CSP will notify the middleware to check and resend the downlink message to ensure user experience.

3.2 Implementation Scheme

According to the above general workflow, the detailed implementation scheme of
the proposed 5GMS middleware is illustrated in Fig. 5 and described as follows.

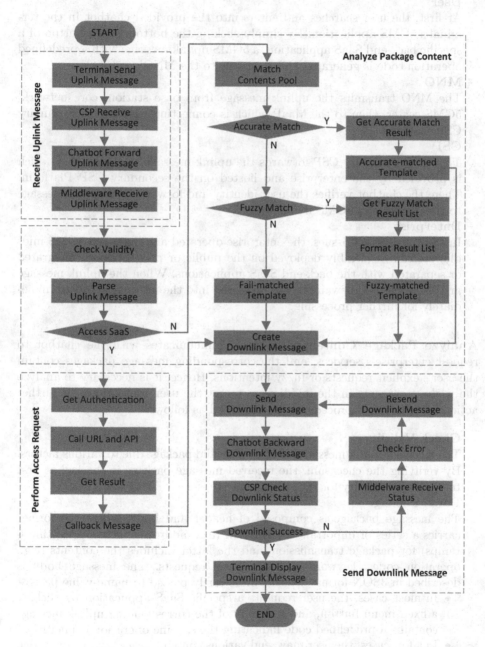

Fig. 5. Implementation scheme of 5GMS middleware

Receive Uplink Message. The uplink message is transmitted along the route of User's terminal, MNO's network, CSP's chatbot, and Enterprise's middleware as follows:

- **User**

  At first, the user searches and enters into the provided chatbot in the terminal's 5GMS application. By simply clicking the bottom menu button of a specific back-end SaaS application, a 5GMS uplink message with a predefined operation code is generated and then sent to the MNO's network.
- **MNO**

  The MNO transmits the uplink message from base station, core network, 5GMS center, then to the MaaP which is connecting with its basic primary CSP platform.
- **CSP**

  The MNO's primary CSP forwards the uplink message to the chatbot which is provided by the enterprise and hosted on the secondary CSP Platform. Then, the chatbot verifies the user identity and forwards the uplink message to the enterprise's 5GMS middleware.
- **Enterprise**

  In view of practical issues, the enterprise operated and managed 5GMS middleware can be flexibly deployed on the public or private cloud, integrated or separated with the back-end SaaS applications. When the uplink message arrives at the middleware, it will be stored into the internal database immediately for further processing.

Analyze Package Content. The user communicates with the chatbot to request enterprise's services, and the corresponding message packages contain the user's explicit requests or fuzzy intentions. Hence, it is necessary to analyze the package contents in the middleware to get the user's intentions for further actions. The detailed procedures are described as follows.

- **Check Validity**

  The received uplink message may be an invalid package due to various factors. By verifying the checksum, the received message package is checked at first to ensure its validity for the subsequent steps.
- **Parse Package**

  The message package is composed of header and body, where the former carries a series of important information (e.g., addresses, certificates, timestamps) for package transmission, and the latter includes the contents (e.g., operation codes, keywords) of the user's requests. The message body is described in JSON format which can be easily parsed to name-value pairs.
  - In most cases, the user requests a specific SaaS application by clicking a fixed menu button, and the body of the corresponding uplink message contains a predefined code indicating the specific operation explicitly.
  - In a few cases, the user may send various contents (e.g., text, symbol, rich media) freely in the 5GMS dialog box, and thus the undefined contents

in the message body should be understood as much as possible firstly to determine the user's real intentions and then to perform further specific operations.

- **Match Intention**

  An enterprise-managed and continuously evolving contents pool, containing massive high-frequency keywords and several confirmation message templates, is adopted to match the user's various intentions.

  - If a user sends a preset keyword accurately in the contents pool, the middleware will match the keyword to its corresponding accurate-matched template.
  - Else if a user sends some fuzzy words in the contents pool, the middleware will match them to a results list assembled in a fuzzy-matched template.
  - Otherwise, if no contents can be matched properly, the middleware will post a fail-matched template.

  Then, the above accurate, fuzzy or fail matched template will be created as a downlink message with button(s) linking with specific SaaS function(s), which will be send back to the user for confirmation.

Following the above procedures, by parsing package directly or matching-confirming contents indirectly, the user's intentions can be analyzed from the received uplink message.

Perform Access Request. When the user's explicit request is determined, the middleware will start the procedures of accessing back-end SaaS applications.

- **Get Authentication**

  The certificate is crucial for the user to access back-end SaaS applications. When first use, the middleware will create and send a downlink message for getting authentication, and the user manually clicks the message button to login the SaaS with account and password. Thus, the SaaS certificate is mapped with the user's telephone number and stored in the middleware's account matching module. The obtained certificate will be auto-refreshed periodically, and the user can access the SaaS application without frequent manual login and authentication.

- **Call URL and API**

  The middleware adopts the above certificate to call URL and API, where the former is the SaaS function entrance and the latter can return specific required results.

- **Callback Message**

  The obtained callback results will be assembled into a downlink message, which will be displayed as a rich-media card with SaaS function buttons and several required data.

Following the above procedures, the user's request can be performed, and the corresponding results will be returned back to the user in the form of a downlink message.

Send Downlink Message. The above confirmation, authentication and call-back results should be assembled into corresponding downlink messages and sent back from middleware, CSP, to the original user.

- **Middleware**
  The middleware is responsible for assembling the internal generated confirmation, authentication and callback results into corresponding downlink message packages, and then sending them back to the CSP platform.
- **CSP**
  The CSP platform is responsible for sending packages to the MNO's network and supervising the sending status reported from MaaP. If the message cannot be returned successfully, the CSP will notify the middleware to check and resend the downlink message until received by the user.
- **User**
  When the package arrives at the user terminal, the native 5GMS application will render it to a rich-media card with SaaS function buttons. When a specific button is tapped, the internal WebView component of the 5GMS application will be called out to display the user interface of the specific SaaS function.

4 Conclusion

The brand-new 5G messaging service is regarded as an ideal entrance for various enterprise-level SaaS applications, where the crucial enabler is the message middleware between the CSP and enterprises. In this paper, we design and implement a 5GMS-to-SaaS middleware to facilitate establishing connections between the unified front-end 5GMS chatbot and a large amount of various back-end SaaS applications. Our proposed 5GMS middleware can deal with practical issues such as message transmission, format conversion, and account matching uniformly, so as to normalize and simplify the procedures of linking massive services. With the help of our proposed middleware, various enterprise-level 5GMS-based SaaS applications can be developed more efficiently, and the corresponding businesses can be expanded more rapidly and extensively as well.

References

1. GSM Doc 28/85: Services and Facilities to be provided in the GSM System (rev2) (1985)
2. GSMA: Rich Communication Services. https://www.gsma.com/futurenetworks/rcs/
3. GSMA RCC.07: Rich Communication Suite - Advanced Communications Services and Client Specification (Version 11.0). GSMA Official Document (2019)
4. GSMA RCC.08: Rich Communications Suite Endorsement of 3GPP TS29.311 Interworking for Messaging Services (Version 9.0). GSMA Official Document (2019)
5. GSMA RCC.10: Rich Communication Suite Endorsement of OMA CPM 2.2 Interworking (Version 9.0). GSMA Official Document (2019)

6. GSMA RCC.11: Rich Communication Suite Endorsement of OMA CPM 2.2 Conversation Functions (Version 9.0). GSMA Official Document (2019)
7. GSMA RCC.71: RCS Universal Profile Service Definition Document (Version 2.4). GSMA Official Document (2019)
8. China Telecom, China Mobile, China Unicom: White Paper on 5G Messaging Services (2020)
9. Clark-Dickson, P.: 5G Messaging Poised to Deliver Ecosystem Innovation. Omdia White Paper (2020)
10. Linux Foundation: Cloud Information Model. https://cloudinformationmodel.org/

Blockchain Developments and Innovations – An Analytical Evaluation of Software Engineering Approaches

Mahdi Fahmideh[1], Anuradha Gunawardana[2], Shiping Chen[3], Jun Shen[2], and Brian Yecies[2(✉)]

[1] University of Southern Queensland, Toowoomba, Australia
Mahdi.Fahmideh@usq.edu.au
[2] University of Wollongong, Wollongong, Australia
{jshen,byecies}@uow.edu.au
[3] CSIRO Data61, Eveleigh, Australia
Shiping.Chen@data61.csiro.au

Abstract. Blockchain has received expanding interest from various domains. Institutions, enterprises, governments, and agencies are interested in Blockchain's potential to augment their software systems. The unique requirements and characteristics of Blockchain platforms raise new challenges involving extensive enhancement to conventional software development processes to meet the needs of these domains. Software engineering approaches supporting Blockchain-oriented developments have been slow to materialize, despite proposals in the literature, and they have yet to be objectively analyzed. A critical appraisal of these innovations is crucial to identify their respective strengths and weaknesses. We present an analytical evaluation of several prominent Blockchain-oriented methods through a comprehensive, criteria-based evaluation framework. The results can be used for comparing, adapting, and developing a new generation of Blockchain-oriented software development processes and innovations.

Keywords: Blockchain · Software engineering · Software development innovations · Evaluation framework

1 Introduction

Based on recent trends and evidence, views on the development of Blockchain technology are diverse and contrasting. A recent global survey by Deloitte [1] found that IT-based organizations are keen to adopt Blockchain and consider adopting it as a priority to improve the performance of their operational systems. Furthermore, Bosu et al. [2] reported the results of a prototype Blockchain project hosted on GitHub that more than doubled in engagement from 3,000 to 6,800 use cases between March and October 2018. The number of related projects launched within this relatively short time demonstrates the allure of this technology among our research community.

© Springer Nature Switzerland AG 2022
B. Tekinerdogan et al. (Eds.): ICIOT 2021, LNCS 12993, pp. 58–76, 2022.
https://doi.org/10.1007/978-3-030-96068-1_5

On the other hand, substantial financial losses caused by numerous attacks and system failures related to Blockchain and smart contract applications are evident in many industry reports. Notable examples include the Coinrail exchange hack in 2018, with the loss of $42 million worth of cryptocurrencies; the DAO attack in 2016, ending in the withdrawal of Ether funds worth $50–60 million; the $65 million loss following the Bitfinex attack in 2016; and the $600 million loss due to the 2014 MtGox attack [3, 4]. To mitigate such failures, adopting systematic software engineering approaches, as acknowledged in several previous studies (e.g., [4, 5]), is essential. A systematic engineering methodology will allow Blockchain developers to design a Blockchain system and implement it in a manageable manner without exposing it to attacks and vulnerabilities. Moreover, unlike an ad-hoc methodology, errors occurring within a systematic approach can be better traced and fixed. A systematic approach will better assist development teams to deal with the uncertainties surrounding Blockchain-oriented software caused by its relative immaturity and the many under-explored areas associated with the technology.

Responding to these issues, in this paper we set up a research agenda to i) review existing advances in Blockchain development; ii) propose an evaluation framework including a coherent set of criteria derived from both the Blockchain and software engineering literature; iii) evaluate the selected development approaches against the criterion set; and iv) outline evaluation outcomes. Hence, our study contributes to Blockchain-oriented software engineering in two major ways:

- By providing an evaluation framework as a useful tool by which to compare and contrast existing Blockchain engineering approaches and to prioritize and select one innovation which fits the requirements of a given Blockchain-oriented system development project.
- By identifying unaddressed knowledge gaps in the innovations relating to Blockchain development in order to map out future research directions.

Section 2 explores the history and background of Blockchian technology and discusses recent work on software engineering for Blockchain-based systems. Section 3 presents a review of a selected set of Blockchain development innovations. Section 4 details the criteria for an evaluation framework, along with an evaluation of existing Blockchian development approaches. In Sect. 5, we discuss the evaluation outcomes reported in the previous section, as well as the limitations of the processes reviewed. Finally, conclusions and suggestions for future work are presented in Sect. 6.

2   Background

2.1   Blockchain

Blockchain technology originated with the introduction of Bitcoin cryptocurrency in 2008 [6]. Since then, industrial interest in Blockchain system development has expanded significantly, with companies exploring the potential of Blockchain-enabled Internet-based systems for the future [7]. Fundamentally, a Blockchain is a cryptographically linked chain of records or blocks, with each block containing a hash value of the previous block and one or more transaction logs with their timestamp [7]. These chains of blocks are stored on a distributed node network, allowing each participant node to retain a copy of the Blockchain. Participating nodes validate each new block by collectively agreeing if the new block can join the existing Blockchain. The process of reaching collective agreement is known as a consensus mechanism. After successful validation, a new block is added to the existing Blockchain. These validating and chaining procedures make these blocks suitable for storing sensitive financial transaction information, as users can rely on a secure exchange of information without needing an intermediary, potentially a less trustworthy mechanism [8].

The ability to create smart contracts is an important attribute of Blockchain technology. Smart contracts are database slots that store the necessary logic to create and validate transactions; these contracts allow users to read, update, and delete data stored in Blockchain systems [6]. These smart contracts can be implemented either via domain-specific languages like Solidity on Ethereum, or using general-purpose languages like Java and Go, which can be familiar to Blockchain developers. Moreover, smart contracts create a pathway for non-Blockchain software systems to integrate Blockchain technology, where the business logic, rules, and data specific to that system are coded into smart contracts which are then executed and deployed in decentralized ledgers. However, the meticulous design and robust development of smart contracts in Blockchain systems are essential to mitigate the effects of malicious attacks and exceptions caused by poorly designed or badly implemented platforms.

2.2 Development of Blockchain-Based Systems

Blockchain-based software engineering is associated with a range of concepts and terminologies. A common understanding of these diverse notions and terms is essential to successful Blockchain system development. According to Porru et al. [4], a Blockchain-based system is a novel software system that utilizes a Blockchain implementation in its components. Thus, innovations across various Blockchain developments can be viewed as an extension of traditional software development, with the need to incorporate features of a Blockchain system such as decentralized architecture, systematic block transaction recording, and data redundancy [6, 9].

As mentioned in Sect. 1, Blockchain development should be based on systematic approaches, characterized by an endorsed collection of phases, activities, practices, tools, documenting, and user training [10], thereby providing clarity about how one should perform each activity prescribed under a given process. Although adopting such methodologies may not necessarily guarantee optimal software quality, as suggested in [11, 12] there is a strong correlation between the quality of a particular engineering innovation and the final software product's performance.

In developing Blockchain systems, developers encounter numerous challenges including, but not limited to, compromise between security and performance, choice of an appropriate consensus mechanism, and the complexities around multiple stakeholder corporations [7, 13]. On top of these challenges, the relative immaturity of Blockchain technology increases the complexity of Blockchain adoption, calling for extra effort from developers used to working on conventional software engineering projects. As pointed out by Ingalls [14] forty years ago, the more complex the system, the more susceptible it is to total breakdown, making it all the more important for developers to follow systematic engineering approaches incorporating the Software Development Life Cycle (SDLC). In this paper, the evaluation framework to be elaborated in Sect. 4 has incorporated the complexities surrounding Blockchain adoption, and its criteria have been developed with a strong focus on the SDLC and recommended systematic software engineering practices.

3 Existing Studies of Blockchain-Based Systems Development

This section briefly describes six prominent Blockchain development innovations, which have been selected based on four key criteria. Thus the approach: i) fully or partially describes the development process of a Blockchain system; ii) is based on all (or at least some) of the SDLC phases; iii) describes all Blockchain's chief integral characteristics discussed in Sect. 2 – for instance, smart contracts and block validation; iv) has been recently published, between January 2018 and December 2020. Based on our investigation of academic papers in line with these criteria, we selected six approaches, namely CBDG [15], BADAO [16], BSDP [17], BSCRE [19], BAFISCT [20], and BCSTM [21]. Since many studies are ongoing, this is an incomplete list. For each of these approaches, we provide a brief description of its development process, focusing on the SDLC phases.

3.1 CBDG

The CBDG approach [15] describes the development tasks required to build a Blockchain system, shown in Fig. 1. As the first task, possible future benefits of integrating Blockchain are identified. In this space, either the existing systems are migrated to a Blockchain-enabled system or a completely new system is developed from scratch. If integrating Blockchain is considered beneficial, the next task is to select a suitable Blockchain implementation platform like Ethereum. The authors of [15] underline the importance of using such a platform as against building a completely new Blockchain, which could potentially involve many years of work.

The third task involves identifying development requirements and defining an appropriate Blockchain model and a conceptual workflow. A range of other related factors – including i) permissions from the Blockchain network, ii) choice of front-end programming languages, iii) external databases, and iv) servers – are also considered. Next, a Proof-of-Concept (PoC) prototype of the Blockchain system is designed to secure client approval. In designing this PoC, client feedback is also incorporated. The formulated prototype consists of various components including i) information architecture, ii) designs, and iii) sketches. Once the PoC is approved by the client, visual and technical designs are completed as the fifth task. These artefacts depict the complete design of the Blockchain system to be developed, and they also incorporate User Interface and API designs. The sixth and final task entails developing the Blockchain system based on the set designs. Here the first development is referred to as the pre-alpha version, as formal testing and client approval have not yet been realized. The pre-alpha version is then subjected to thorough testing and moves through three more versions, alpha, beta, and finally the Release Candidate version. At the end of this process, the fully tested

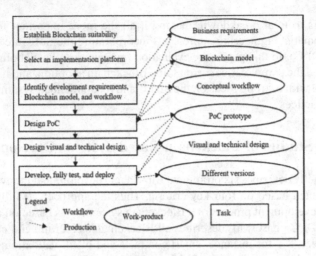

Fig. 1. CBDG approach block diagram

system is deployed. Importantly, the deployed Blockchain system should be able to be upgraded when required.

3.2 BADAO

The BADAO approach [16] describes a model-based, process-driven method for developing a Blockchain-enabled system – either a Decentralized Autonomous Organization (DAO) or Block-chain-Augmented Organization (BAO). In a DAO, the traditional centralized transaction processing is decentralized and automated via smart contracts. In the case of BAOs, they are identified as or-ganizations, and are augmented with Blockchain features such as immutability and traceability.

Figure 2 illustrates the development tasks germane to the BADAO approach. Firstly, a Business Process Model (BPM) for the desired business scenario is defined. This BPM guides the subsequent development process based on SDLC phases. The next task involves establishing the suitability of Blockchain for the identified business case, expressed as either DAO-suitable, BAO-suitable, or not suitable. If BAO is found to be suitable, the process boundaries of the BAO are determined. Here, consideration is given to automating as many processes as possible utilizing Blockchain and smart contracts, while allowing non-Blockchain processes to complement Blockchain-enabled ones.

After completing these tasks, the construction of a Platform Independent Model (PIM) is undertaken. This model is independent of any features specific to a particular Blockchain platform. However, the PIM includes features such as smart contract architectures, Blockchain state definitions, and security models attached to the Blockchain model. Next, a Platform Specific Model (PSM) is constructed to incorporate elements relevant to the Blockchain platform selected. The realized PSM can be used to implement the Blockchain solution once the smart contracts are implemented and the design concepts are validated.

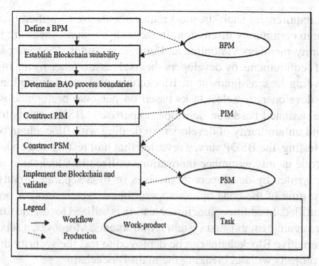

Fig. 2. BADAO approach block diagram

3.3 BSDP

BSDP [17] has undertaken an online survey of 1604 Blockchain developers in 145 Blockchain projects hosted on GitHub. The survey asked about the different methods utilized by Blockchain developers in conducting requirement analysis, tasks assignment, testing, and verification of Blockchain projects. These development tasks are depicted in Fig. 3.

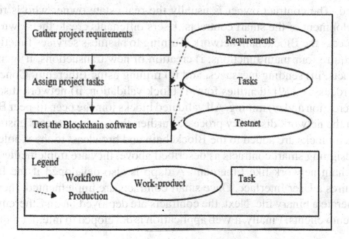

Fig. 3. BSDP approach block diagram

In terms of requirement analysis, most requirements are identified by project managers and through community discussion. In these discussions, ideas are brainstormed among community members via online and offline meetings. Customer feedback and the selection of requirements by developers themselves are other forms of requirement analysis. Regarding task assignment in Blockchain projects, few options are identified. Allowing developers to select tasks based on personal preference is one option. Some tasks are assigned based on developer expertise – BSDP points to the relative inexperience and unfamiliarity of developers in dealing with Blockchain projects.

Regarding testing, the BSDP survey revealed that unit testing and code review were the two main code quality assurance innovations utilized in Blockchain projects. Unit tests are either written by developers themselves or by a separate quality assessment team. Manual testing of the code by developers themselves is another popular testing mechanism identified. In addition, functional testing is utilized to test the functionality of the end software against established system requirements. Moreover, a separate Testnet, which is an alternative Blockchain, can be deployed to test the security and scalability of Blockchain projects without breaking the main Blockchain.

3.4 BSCRE

BSCRE describes the design and implementation of a Blockchain system in the real-estate industry [19]. A graphical overview of BSCRE's development tasks is provided in Fig. 4. Firstly, the requirements of the proposed Blockchain system are gathered. Next, the design of smart contracts involves three main steps: i) formulating actors and their role definitions, ii) defining business service functions, and iii) describing Ethereum processes.

Regarding actors and their roles, two main actors named as contract owner and users are identified. The contract owner is usually the real-estate owner who is responsible for the development of the smart contracts. Users or tenants create their own Ethereum wallets to access the Blockchain network. Turning to business services functions, smart contracts require four main functions: i) creation of new transactions, ii) generation of smart contracts, iii) sending messages, and iv) mining using Ethereum. Concerning the Ethereum processes, [19] identifies four: i) block validation, ii) network discovery, iii) transaction creation and iv) mining. All validated blocks join the peer-to-peer Blockchain network via the network discovery process. Further, the mining process ensures that all new validated blocks are added to the Blockchain and broadcast to the whole network.

After designing smart contracts as described above, they are implemented on a suitable Blockchain network like Ethereum. A dapp is also developed if the Blockchain system requires a User Interface. Once smart contracts are implemented, they are compiled to generate a binary file. Next, the contracts are deployed on an Ethereum network using Ethereum clients. Finally, a Web application is developed to interact with the smart contracts.

3.5 BAFISCT

BAFISCT describes a development process designed to integrate Blockchain with supply chain processes [20]. The tasks associated with BAFISCT's development process are shown in Fig. 5. Firstly, the target product for the supply chain operations is defined. This is followed by the identification of the characteristics of the selected product. These product characteristics include a range of factors – for instance, the producer, price, and design of the product. The third task entails identifying all the requirements attached to the product, which can be functional, regulatory, or technical. Based on these requirements, the main actors involved in supply chain processes relevant to the selected product are defined as the fourth task. Next, the different operations and processes attached to these actors are identified and modelled as *Block Flow Diagrams*.

Following this step, the business rules relevant to the product and its operations are defined. These rules are included in the Blockchain, and will be appropriately executed to process supply chain transactions relevant to the product. Next, the different digital assets relevant to supply chain processes are also defined. Following this, the information flow within the identified digital assets and processes are defined. Once the information flow is recognized, a complete view of a Blockchain transaction in terms of the information processed and its subsequent outcome on Blockchain can be observed.

The next task, configuration of Blockchain, involves i) identification of a suitable Blockchain network (permissioned or permission-less), ii) selecting a suitable consensus mechanism and a Blockchain platform, iii) designing User Interfaces, and iv) developing APIs. Finally, testing of the configured Blockchain via unit and integration tests is performed.

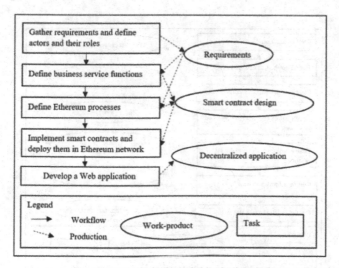

Fig. 4. BSCRE approach block diagram

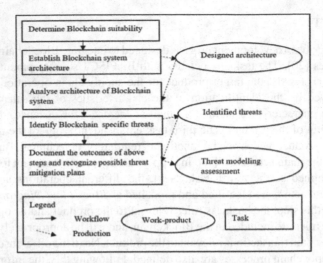

Fig. 5. BAFISCT approach block diagram

3.6 BCSTM

The BCSTM approach introduced by [21] is designed to be used in conducting a security assessment of Blockchain-enabled software architecture. For that purpose, it identifies a range of Blockchain-specific security threats and, based on these threats, the selected architecture is evaluated utilizing the popular STRIDE threat-modelling approach [22]. Figure 6 illustrates the development tasks associated with the BCSTM approach.

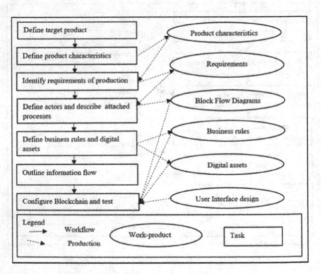

Fig. 6. BCSTM approach block diagram

Firstly, [21] discusses a range of factors that impact the suitability of Blockchain for a given scenario. Here, among many other factors, Blockchain features such as immutability, and basic Blockchain functions such as block validation, are also considered. After establishing Blockchain suitability, the next task is to define a Blockchain architecture and select an appropriate Blockchain implementation. For implementation, a suitable network – for instance, a permissioned network – should be selected. Further, regarding data storage, [21] describes three possible options. These are *hash*, where only the hash value of a data item is stored on Blockchain; *generic*, for all non-hash data storage; and *smart contract*, for the storage of executable code.

Next, Blockchain-specific threats relevant to the selected Blockchain architecture are identified. In [21] eight separate categories have been identified to indicate the range of these threats; smart contract, cryptocurrency, and permissioned ledger threats are a few of the categories considered. Finally, based on these listed threats, a threat-modelling assessment is conducted to generate a holistic view of Blockchain security. In this assessment, possible threat mitigation actions and decisions are also recognized and documented.

4 Criteria-Based Evaluation

4.1 Evaluation Framework

Our developed evaluation framework is structured to review existing Blockchain approaches, and to classify, evaluate, and characterize their innovations based on accepted software engineering practices. In so doing, we have followed two main steps as described below.

Step I. Defining meta-level characteristics: Meta-characteristics are features that are anticipated will be satisfied by an ideal evaluation framework. It is essential to have a set of meta-characteristics to guide the selection of appropriate criteria for the framework, as they can be used to evaluate different criteria and decide whether they should be added to the framework. For the purpose of our framework, we extracted five meta-characteristics defined in [23]. These characteristics are i) preciseness, for creating unambiguous, quantifiable, and descriptive criteria; ii) simplicity, for ease of understanding; iii) soundness, for the relation or semantic link between the criterion and the problem domain; iv) minimal overlapping, for distinct and minimally interdependent criteria; and v) generality, to ensure the abstract character of criteria independent of specific details, standards, and technologies.

Step II. Derivation of the criteria set: We reviewed existing evaluation frameworks such as [23, 25, 26], as well as more recent Blockchain literature, to derive a set of criteria which are applicable to Blockchain development and also satisfy the meta-characteristics defined in step I above. Following an iterative refinement and elimination of duplicated criteria, a list of eighteen criteria was derived. Table 1 briefly describes each of these eighteen criteria, which were utilized to evaluate all the approaches evaluated in Sect. 3.

Table 1. Evaluation criteria

Criteria description/evaluation questions (Letter C uniquely identifies the criteria)	
Criteria related to the analysis phase	
Analysing context (C1): Does the approach describe factors that are used to determine suitability of integrating Blockchain with a software system?	**Requirement analysis (C2):** Does the approach describe or refer to a requirement-gathering process, techniques, or methods?
Criteria related to the design phase	
Smart contract design (C3): Does the approach describe or refer to a smart contract design process? Is the functionality of a smart contract described?	**Consensus mechanism (C4):** Does the approach refer to a consensus protocol used and/or describe a functionality in a Blockchain system?
Architecture design (C5): Does the approach describe the overall architecture of a Blockchain system? Has the proposed architecture been segregated into multiple layers?	**Security (C6):** Is there any discussion of enhancing or maintaining security of a Blockchain system and architecture design requirements?
Privacy (C7): Is there any discussion of how the privacy of user data is protected, or are there references to privacy risks, guidelines or policies applicable to a Blockchain system?	
Criteria related to the implementation and testing phase	
Testing (C8): What is the nature of the support, in terms of techniques and recommendations, provided by the approach in testing functional and non-functional operations?	
Criteria related to tool support	
Tools (C9): Is there any evidence of third-party or custom-made tools that can be used to speed up or automate tasks being followed in development of a Blockchain system?	
Criteria related to the deployment phase	
Deployment mechanism (C10): Does the approach refer to deployment of a Blockchain system? Is there any evidence of configuration of hardware and/or software components that are needed for deployment?	
Criteria related to modelling	
Modelling language (C11): Has the approach included one or more representational languages used at design and/or run time of a Blockchain system?	**Work products (C12):** Is there any evidence of one or more interim project outputs/artefacts applicable to each SDLC development phase?
Criteria related to user support and training	
Training (C13): Is there any evidence of training manuals, user documentation, or other forms of support and guidance to develop a Blockchain system?	**Procedures and supportive techniques (C14):** Does the approach include algorithms or step-by-step guidance to follow or practice tasks required to develop a Blockchain system? Is there any evidence of supportive techniques or examples related to development tasks?

(continued)

Table 1. (*continued*)

Other criteria	
Scalability (C15): Does the approach describe techniques/factors that allow a Blockchain system to scale up to handle high volumes of transactions and data requests, or refer to scalability testing mechanisms?	**Blockchain type (C16):** Does the approach identify or suggest a suitable Blockchain network for a Blockchain system?
Domain applicability (C17): Is the approach directed towards one or more industries or domains?	**Development roles (C18):** Does the approach define or describe different roles required to develop a Blockchain system?

The criteria selected span eight categories. Four cover the 'analysis', 'design', 'testing and implementation', and 'deployment' phases of the SDLC. Two criteria, modelling language and work products, are associated with the 'modelling' category since they capture different representational languages and models applicable to Blockchain development. The 'user support and training' category includes criteria that provide support and guidance for developers to create a Blockchain system. Unsurprisingly, the tool criterion comes under the 'tool support' category. Finally, four additional criteria are classified under the 'other' category, exceptional features which address other elements anticipated in a Blockchain development approach. Although we are not suggesting that our framework covers all possible criteria relevant to Blockchain development, we believe that such a comprehensive framework is not found in the existing Blockchain literature.

4.2 Evaluation Outcomes

In Table 2, the evaluation outcomes of the six Blockchain approaches based on 15 scaled criteria are summarized. The scaled criteria are based on a five-point Likert Scale: fully supported, considerably supported, moderately supported, slightly supported, and not supported. Three remaining criteria, C16, C17, and C18, are descriptive in nature, as the answers to them are more open-ended. Hence, they are not evaluated based on the scale. For C16, the type of Blockchain network supported under each process is reviewed. For C17, the target domain of each approach is scrutinized. For C18, a distinct list of development roles applicable to Blockchain development are extracted from the selected innovations.

Table 2. Evaluation outcomes

Criteria	Approach					
	CBDG	BADAO	BSDP	BSCRE	BAFISCT	BCSTM
C1	●	◕	○	◔	○	●
C2	◓	◔	●	◕	◓	◔
C3	◔	◓	◔	●	○	◓
C4	◓	◔	◔	◓	◕	●
C5	◓	◓	◔	●	●	◕
C6	●	◓	●	◔	◔	●
C7	◔	◔	○	◔	◔	●
C8	●	○	●	○	●	○
C9	●	◓	●	◔	◓	○
C10	●	○	◔	◓	○	○
C11	○	●	○	◓	◓	◓
C12	●	◓	◓	◓	●	◓
C13	○	○	◓	○	◔	◔
C14	◓	◓	●	◓	●	●
C15	○	○	●	○	◔	◓

●	Fully supported
◕	Considerably supported
◓	Moderately supported
◔	Slightly supported
○	Not supported

5   Criteria-Based Evaluation

5.1   Findings

In this section, we briefly discuss the findings related to each criterion of our evaluation framework. For the 15 scaled criteria, the discussion is based on the evaluation outcomes reported in Table 2.

Analyzing context (C1) – Due to the complexity surrounding Blockchain-enabled software development, a range of innovations should provide clear guidance in establishing the suitability of Blockchain for a given software system. Only the BCSTM and CBDG approaches fully satisfy this criterion. BCSTM and CBDG review a range of factors to establish Blockchain suitability [15, 21] including i) the requirement to store users' personal information on Blockchain itself; ii) the need to update the rules of the software system; iii) rewarding or compensating participating nodes; iv) the number of nodes required to validate new blocks; and v) required transaction speed. Furthermore, BSDP and BAFISCT fail to provide any information about this criterion.

Requirement analysis (C2) – identifies the functional and non-functional require-ments that need to be fulfilled by a Blockchain system. Further, approaches may provide descriptions of supporting techniques, such as interviews and workshops, which can be used to gather requirements. BSDP is the only method to fully satisfy this criterion. It describes the different techniques used to gather Blockchain project requirements based on the findings of a survey of Blockchain projects hosted on GitHub. These techniques are briefly summarized in Sect. 3 under the review of the BSDP approach. Additionally, BSCRE considerably supported this criterion, as BSCRE mentions conducting orga-nizational workshops and gathering requirements from the different stakeholders of a company. Notably, none of the reviewed methods achieved a rating of not supported.

Smart contract design (C3) – is an integral part of a Blockchain system. If they are not meticulously designed, the whole Blockchain system is susceptible to malicious external attacks. Only BSCRE was able to fully satisfy this criterion. The main steps include i) redefining actors based on their direct interaction with the smart contracts; ii) defining smart contract decomposition; iii) defining message flows and data structure; iv) defining modifiers (special functions called before other functions) and internal func-tions; and v) defining tests and security assessment procedures [19]. BSCRE provides a comprehensive smart contract design process, which is discussed under the BSCRE approach segment in Sect. 3. BAFISCT is the only method to provide an absence of details on smart contract design.

Consensus mechanism (C4) – ensures that new blocks are only added to the Blockchain network once majority nodes agree and verify them. Although the role of a consensus mechanism is referred to in five out of the six reviewed approaches, only BCSTM achieved a rating of fully supported. Accordingly, the role of a consen-sus protocol is more critical in a permission-less network, as anyone can participate in its transaction validation process. Also in BCSTM is the need to continuously pro-vide adequate financial compensation for all nodes participating in block validation in a permission-less network. If nodes are not adequately compensated, the block validation process will not run at optimum efficiency, which could result in malicious attacks on the Blockchain system. The alternative consideration to this problem is to use a permis-sioned network where the number of participating nodes is controlled [21]. Furthermore, the BAFISCT approach states that the chosen consensus mechanism should be compat-ible with the Blockchain platform or framework, such as Ethereum, on top of which the Blockchain system is to be developed.

Architecture design (C5) – of a Blockchain system provides evidence of how each component of the system is positioned relative to the other components. Architecture can also be described according to multiple layers. As Table 2 shows, two approaches fully satisfied this criterion, while no single approach was rated as not supported. A brief description of the Blockchain architecture utilized in each approach is provided in Sect. 3.

Security (C6) – Security is an important dimension associated with Blockchain sys-tems. Of the reviewed innovations, only BSDP and BCSTM fully satisfy this criterion.

As elaborated in Sect. 3, BCSTM proposes a threat modelling process designed to conduct a security assessment of a Blockchain-enabled software architecture. The outcomes of this threat-modelling assessment provide valuable insights into the level of security evident in the architecture of a given Blockchain. Moreover, BSDP has discovered that most Blockchain projects incorporate popular code quality assurance mechanisms such as unit testing and code review to test the security of a Blockchain system. It also mentions that bug bounty, static program analysis, simulation, and external audit [17] are used in this regard.

Privacy (C7) – Privacy of user data stored on Blockchain is another important dimension of Blockchain systems. Processes should consider widely accepted standards, rules, and policies on user data privacy when designing Blockchain systems. However, the reviewed approaches provide minimal details about this criterion. The BCSTM approach, which achieved a rating of considerably supported, is the highest rated. According to BCSTM, users' personal information should not be stored on public elements of the Blockchain as it can violate their privacy rights. Furthermore, malfunctions and defects in smart contracts can expose private user data to unauthorized parties [21]. Notably, as Table 2 shows, two approaches fail to provide any details about Blockchain privacy.

Testing (C8) – The testing mechanism describes the techniques and recommendations provided by the methods to test functional and non-functional operations of a Blockchain system. While three out of the six reviewed approaches fully satisfy this criterion, three others did not provide any details on testing. The testing mechanism associated with each supporting process is briefly described in Sect. 3.

Tools (C9) – External third-party tools or custom tools can be used to automate or speed up the tasks involved in developing a Blockchain system. Except for BCSTM, all the approaches provide evidence of tool support. However, only CBDG fully supported this criterion, describing a wide range of tools that can be used to automate different Blockchain development tasks. For instance, the Truffle Ethereum framework can be used in developing dapps, and can also serve as a testing framework. Furthermore, the Solium tool is used to format code written in Solidity, and fix security issues in the code.

Deployment mechanism (C10) – The deployment of Blockchain systems can become complex as it requires the configuration of both hardware and software components. Further, the system should be fully tested before being deployed to a production environment. The reviewed approaches provide minimal details on deploying Blockchain systems, with three achieving a rating of not supported. CBDG is the only fully supported approach. Among other elements, it states that the deployed system should be able to receive upgrades in accordance with business requirements. It also mentions various tools that can automate deployment-related tasks. For instance, Remix IDE is a tool that can be used to deploy smart contracts. BSCRE mentions deploying implemented smart contracts to an Ethereum network using Ethereum clients, Geth and PyEthApp [19]. BSDP also refers to the deployment of a fully tested system despite failing to provide detailed descriptions.

Modelling language (C11) – A modelling language can be used to represent different work products in a Blockchain development innovation in a structured manner. Apart from two approaches, as Table 2 shows, the selected processes have all utilized some form of modelling language. However, only BADAO fully supported this criterion.

Work products (C12) – Work products are the interim project deliverables that can be identified from a Blockchain development process. All the reviewed methods incorporated at least one work product, and no approach received a rating lower than moderately supported. In Sect. 3, we have modelled the work products relevant to each approach in block diagrams as shown in Fig. 1, 2, 3, 4, 5 and 6.

Training (C13) – Procedures should provide training, in terms of training manuals, user documentation, and other forms of support and guidance necessary to develop a Blockchain system. To our knowledge, none of the six reviewed approaches provides comprehensive details of training. This might be a serious limitation that needs to be considered by potential practitioners and researchers in the future. Nevertheless, a few of the lines of action provide partial support for this criterion. For instance, BCSTM supports documenting evaluation outcomes of its threat modelling assessment.

Procedures and supportive techniques (C14) – Step-by-step guidelines or an appropriate algorithm might assist developers to better understand the various development tasks described in a Blockchain innovation. In addition, some helpful examples, or supportive techniques designed to undertake these tasks might also be provided. All six reviewed approaches, as Table 2 shows, provide some level of support for this criterion. However, only three approaches achieved the highest rating.

Scalability (C15) –The ability of a Blockchain system to handle large volumes of data and transactions is a sign of its high scalability. However, only the BSDP approach fully satisfied this criterion, as it discusses a range of relevant testing techniques, such as stress testing. Otherwise, while a few strategies refer to scalability issues in Blockchain systems, none provides any details of possible mechanisms to mitigate them. Four of the reviewed approaches failed to provide any details on scalability.

Blockchain type (C16) – Table 3 identifies the supporting Blockchain network types.

Domain applicability (C17) Table 3 identifies the applicable arena for each approach.

Development roles (C18) – describe the duties and responsibilities of different IT professionals participating in a Blockchain system. However, development role definitions are limited in existing approaches. Table 5 summarizes the identified development roles.

Table 3. Blockchain type

Approach	Blockchain network type		
	Permission-less	Permissioned	Not stated
CBDG			✓
BADAO		✓	
BSDP			✓
BSCRE		✓	
BAFISCT			✓
BCSTM		✓	

Table 4. Domain applicability

Approach	Domain
BAFISCT	Supply chain
BSCRE	Real estate
BCSTM, BSDP, CBDG, BADAO	Not stated or multiple domains

Table 5. Development roles

Role	Referred approaches	Description
Smart contract owner	BSCRE	Responsibilities to create, compile, and deploy smart contracts
Software engineer	BADAO	To perform software engineering roles in developing a Blockchain-oriented software
Blockchain developer	BCSTM, CBDG, BADAO, BSDP	To implement Blockchain design models and code smart contracts
Quality assurance	BSDP	Quality checking/testing of Blockchain software
Project lead	BSDP	Overseeing a Blockchain project, and define project requirements when needed

5.2 Limitations

Based on the level of support for the criteria set for our evaluation framework, we identified a number of limitations among existing Blockchain development approaches.

Firstly, previous studies have raised concerns regarding the lack of a comprehensive development methodology to guide the development of Blockchain-based systems. Based on evaluation outcomes reported in Table 2 and the individual analytical analysis in Sect. 3 above, existing Blockchain development approaches limit their focus to a few selected SDLC phases, and their descriptions of Blockchain adoption are generally below the level expected of a full-scale methodology.

Secondly, existing approaches and methods provide very low support for training. Due to this limitation, developers, especially those without experience, following these approaches may cause problems that might result in poorly developed Blockchain systems.

Similarly, there is minimal support for the deployment phase of the SDLC. Existing approaches show little interest in deploying a fully tested Blockchain system, despite deployment being a complex phase requiring proper guidance.

Further, the selected innovations failed to define many of the development roles applicable to Blockchain development, and we were only able to extract five roles (see Table 5).

Last but not least, there is inadequate discussion about protecting the privacy of user data. Since global regulators consider user data privacy a priority, the approaches examined should have given more attention to this issue.

6 Conclusions and Future Work

This paper underlines the need for systematic engineering approaches and innovations to develop Blockchain systems. As a first attempt to fill this need, we presented a descriptive and comprehensive review of six existing Blockchain development approaches in the context of a proposed evaluation framework. Our results highlighted both the strengths and shortcoming of existing approaches; areas for further improvement include phases, activities, practices, tools, documenting, and user training [10]. Future Blockchain applications should incorporate these requirements into their development process so as to ensure both the security and quality of the target Blockchain-oriented software.

Given these findings, a clear research direction for future investigations is the development of a comprehensive Blockchain software engineering innovation that would draw on the strengths of existing approaches, while avoiding their weaknesses. This broad aim can be achieved by extracting method fragments from older processes found in [e.g. 18, 26], as well as from existing Blockchain development approaches, and amalgamating them to create a fully-fledged methodology. Once crafted, the newer and more innovative approach can be customized and improved to accommodate the requirements of different Blockchain systems. Despite the unlikelihood of a single standard or agreement being reached in the future, this effort calls for cooperative work from experts in different fields.

References

1. Pawczuk, L., Massey, R., Holdowsky, J.: Deloitte's 2019 global Blockchain survey - Blockchain gets down to business (2019). https://www2.deloitte.com/content/dam/Deloitte/se/Documents/risk/DI_2019-global-blockchain-survey.pdf
2. Bosu, A., Iqbal, A., Shahriyar, R., Chakraborty, P.: Understanding the motivations, challenges and needs of Blockchain software developers: a survey. Empir. Softw. Eng. 24(4), 2636–2673 (2019)
3. Bratspies, R.: Cryptocurrency and the myth of the trustless transaction. SSRN Electron. J. 25(1), 2–54 (2018)
4. Porru, S., Pinna, A., Marchesi, M., Tonelli, R.: Blockchain-oriented software engineering: challenges and new directions. In: 2017 IEEE/ACM 39th International Conference on Software Engineering Companion (ICSE-C), pp. 169–171 (2017)
5. Al-Mazrouai, G., Sudevan, S.: Managing Blockchain projects with agile methodology. In: Vijayakumar, V., Neelanarayanan, V., Rao, P., Light, J. (eds.) Proceedings of 6th International Conference on Big Data and Cloud Computing Challenges. SIST, vol. 164, pp. 179–187. Springer, Singapore (2020). https://doi.org/10.1007/978-981-32-9889-7_14

6. Crosby, M., Pattanayak, P., Verma, S., Kalyanaraman, V.J.A.I.: Blockchain technology: beyond Bitcoin. Appl. Innov **2**(6–10), 6–15 (2016)
7. Zheng, Z., Xie, S., Dai, H.-N., Chen, X., Wang, H.: 'Blockchain challenges and opportunities: a survey.' Int. J. Web Grid Serv. **14**(4), 352–375 (2018)
8. Guo, Y., Liang, C.: Blockchain application and outlook in the banking industry. Fin. Innov. **2**(1), 1–12 (2016). https://doi.org/10.1186/s40854-016-0034-9
9. Pilkington, M.: Blockchain technology: principles and applications. In: Handbook of Research on Digital Transformations, pp. 1–38. Edward Elgar Publishing, London (2015)
10. Avison, D., Fitzgerald, G.: Information Systems Development: Methodologies, Techniques and Tools, 3rd edn. McGraw-Hill, New York (2003)
11. Cugola, G., Ghezzi, C.: Software processes: a retrospective and a path to the future. Softw. Process Improv. Pract. **4**(3), 101–123 (1998)
12. Fuggetta, A.: 'Software process: a roadmap. In: Proceedings of the Conference on the Future of Software Engineering, Limerick, Ireland, pp. 25–34 (2000)
13. Risius, M., Spohrer, K.: A Blockchain research framework: what we (don't) know, where we go from here, and how we will get there. Bus. Inf. Syst. Eng. **59**(6), 385–409 (2017)
14. Ingalls, D.H.H.: The Smalltalk-76 programming system design and implementation. In: Proceedings of the 5th ACM SIGACT-SIGPLAN symposium on Principles of programming languages - POPL 1978, pp. 9–16 (1978)
15. Takyar, A.: A complete guide to Blockchain development. Leewayhertz.com. https://www.leewayhertz.com/blockchain-development/. Accessed 22 Oct 2019
16. Yue, K.-B.: Blockchain-augmented organizations. In: AMCIS 2020 Proceedings, 2020, pp. 1–9 (3030)
17. Chakraborty, P., Shahriyar, R., Iqbal, A., Bosu, A.: Understanding the software development practices of Bockchain projects: a survey. In: Proceedings of the 12th ACM/IEEE International Symposium on Empirical Software Engineering and Measurement, pp. 1–10. ACM, New York (2018)
18. Harmsen, F., Brinkkernper, S., Oei, H,: Situational method engineering for information system projects. In: Proceedings of the IFIP WG8.1 Working Conference CRIS'94 Maastricht, pp. 169–194 (1994)
19. Karamitsos, I., Papadaki, M., Barghuthi, N.B.A.: Design of the Blockchain smart contract: a use case for real estate. J. Inf. Secur. **09**(03), 177–190 (2018)
20. Bettín-Díaz, R., Rojas, A.E., Mejía-Moncayo, C.: Methodological approach to the definition of a Blockchain system for the food industry supply chain traceability in Computational Science and Its Applications – ICCSA 2018, pp. 19–33. Springer International Publishing, Cham (2018)
21. Hebert, C., Di Cerbo, F.: Secure Blockchain in the enterprise: a methodology. Perv. Mobile Comput. **59,** 101038 (2019)
22. Shostack, A.: Experiences threat modeling at Microsoft. In: Modeling Security Workshop, Dept. of Computing, Lancaster University (2008)
23. Fahmideh, M., et al.: Cloud migration process—a survey, evaluation framework, and open challenges. J. Syst. Softw. **120**, 31–69 (2016)
24. Ramsin, R., Paige, R.F.: Process-centered review of object oriented software development methodologies. ACM Comput. Surv. **40**(1), 1–89 (2008)
25. Sturm, A., Shehory, O.: A framework for evaluating agent-oriented methodologies. In: Agent-Oriented Information Systems, pp. 94–109. Springer, Berlin Heidelberg (2004)
26. Brinkkemper, S.: Method engineering: engineering of information systems development methods and tools. Inf. Softw. Technol. **38**(4), 275–280 (1996)

SimuMan: A Simultaneous Real-Time Method for Representing Motions and Emotions of Virtual Human in Metaverse

Mingmin Zhang[1], Yuan Wang[2], Jiehan Zhou[3], and Zhigeng Pan[2]([⊠])

[1] Zhejiang University, Hangzhou, China
Zhangmm95@zju.edu.cn
[2] Hangzhou Normal University, Hangzhou, China
zgpan@hznu.edu.cn
[3] University of Oulu, Oulu, Finland
jiehan.zhou@ieee.org

Abstract. Metaverse is the next generation gaming Internet, and virtual humans play an important role in Metaverse. The simultaneous representation of motions and emotions of virtual humans attracts more attention in academics and industry, which significantly improves user experience with the vivid continuous simulation of virtual humans. Different from existing work which only focuses on either the expression of facial expressions or body motions, this paper presents a novel and real-time virtual human prototyping system, which enables a simultaneous real-time expression of motions and emotions of virtual humans (short for SimuMan). SimuMan not only enables users to generate personalized virtual humans in the metaverse world, but also enables them to naturally and simultaneously present six facial expressions and ten limb motions, and continuously generate various facial expressions by setting parameters. We evaluate SimuMan objectively and subjectively to demonstrate its fidelity, naturalness, and real-time. The experimental results show that the SimuMan system is characterized by low latency, good interactivity, easy operation, good robustness, and wide application.

Keywords: Metaverse · Virtual human · Facial expression · Motion generation and synthesis · Motion synchronization

1 Introduction

Metaverse is the next generation gaming Internet. Virtual human as the avatar of a real human in metaverse world, can enhance the user's immersion with the help of human-computer interaction by mirroring the user's motions and emotions. How to easily generate a personalized virtual human, how to mirror a real human's motions and emotions to a virtual human become hot research problems in academic and industry of virtual reality.

There are methods to track motions of real human joints by using active sensors [1−3], which capture body motions through various sensors attached on human body

© Springer Nature Switzerland AG 2022
B. Tekinerdogan et al. (Eds.): ICIOT 2021, LNCS 12993, pp. 77–89, 2022.
https://doi.org/10.1007/978-3-030-96068-1_6

and analyze motions according to specific algorithms. These methods are not only expensive, but also have poor user experience, and are easily affected by setting changes. To overcome the limitations of a tracking system with sensor markers, researchers have developed a marker-free motion capturing method which uses multiple cameras to track human motions in general scenes [4, 5]. At present, the most widely used method is to use cameras to obtain image sequences for extracting motions in real-time [6, 7].

The estimation of skeletal poses with one monocular camera has many serious abnormal problems. Motion tracking based on neural networks (NN) can recognize human poses and solve the occlusion problem in different degrees [8, 9]. The NN-based method is better than Kinect, but it is much more time-consuming [7].

3D face reconstruction can be divided into controllable and non-controllable face reconstruction. The controllable one refers to the method for tracking and reconstructing facial expressions with conditions of lighting and camera parameters. Huang et al. [10] used 100 sparse landmarks attached on human face to capture facial expressions with twelve cameras. The system can realize not only facial deformation but also wrinkle details. However, this method requires face reconstruction in a controllable condition with sophisticated instruments and limited application.

The uncontrollable one refers to the method for realizing 3D face reconstruction without knowing camera parameters and lighting conditions, which does not need sophisticated instruments. Booth et al. [11, 12] studied a priori knowledge of facial expressions through scanned images, and reduced the data dimensionality. This method can reconstruct a deformable face. Li et al. [13] proposed the FLAME model, which can generate various individual faces, and has good generalization. Yao et al. [14] proposed a position map regression network (PRN) to realize face reconstruction through multi-task learning. Wu et al. [15] proposed an approach to regress 3DMM parameters from multi-view inputs with an end-to-end trainable Convolutional Neural Network (CNN).

Most existing studies only focuses on either facial expressions or body motions, but a virtual human needs to completely represent both facial expressions and body motions. Pavlakos et al. [16] presented a method for predicting human motions and facial expressions through neural networks, but this method is not real-time. Roth et al. [17] proposed a virtual human system, which combines various elements to construct a complete virtual human. Similar to Pavlakos' work, Roth et al. also developed a real-time virtual human system for completely representing both facial expressions and body motions. Moreover, the system can generate individual human faces.

The main contribution of this paper is as follows:

(1) Present SimuMan framework, a simultaneous real-time method for representing motions and emotions of virtual humans in metaverse. The terms emotion and facial expression will be used interchangeably below.
(2) SimuMan enables to completely represent both facial expressions and body motions simultaneously to generate individual virtual humans.
(3) SimuMan enables to steplessly and consistently transform emotions and body poses of virtual human according to scene changes with our developed multi-modal description language for emotional markers and limb motion description
(4) SimuMan presents users with a natural and smooth representation of real human's facial expressions and limb movements in a way of temporal and spatial coherence.

2 System Framework

Figure 1 illustrates the SimuMan framework, which consists of five modules of Facial Expression, Mannequin, 3D Human Animation, Real-Time Detection, and Render [5].

The Facial Expression module generates a personalized 3D face model by tracking 68 facial feature points. According to the MPEG-4 standard [18, 19], six emotions are generated, such as sadness, surprise, happiness, anger, enjoyed, and neutral expressions. In addition, we can create a new emotion expression by changing parameters.

The Mannequin module makes the use of **MakeHuman** software to generate a human body model, adjusting human body height, hair, and clothing attributes, and exporting an animation model format. In order to be compatible with facial expressions, this module can also add the generated expressions to the animation model. The extended model can adapt to the change of human motions and emotions.

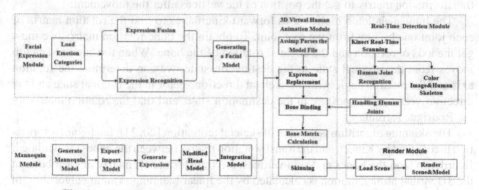

Fig. 1. SimuMan framework (virtual human with emotions and motions)

The 3D Virtual Human Animation Module reconstructs virtual human based on the data on real human's motions obtained by Kinect, realizes the movement of virtual human, and generates emotion animation based on the data captured for facial expressions with the use of Assimp library to parse the files of animation model, binding captured data on bones by Kinect to the bones of a human model, calculating the rotation matrix of bones and skins.

The Real-Time Detection module uses Kinect to capture human joints and uses color video for driving human animation. Kinect scans human skeletons in real-time and outputs color video images synchronously, which is convenient for real-time skeleton tracking. The data on human skeleton includes the coordinates of 25 joints. To eliminate the impact of the jitter caused by Kinect, the stability processing module optimizes the skeleton detection before using the skeleton data to drive the 3D virtual human model.

The Render module consists of the rendering of scene and virtual human.

3 Continuous Emotion Transformation and Its Relevant Motions

3.1 Human Skeleton Motions and Skinning

The movement of bones changes the position of skin vertices on the body model and generates the animation effect of a virtual human. The main idea on body animation is to construct a skeleton that conforms to the anatomical level and use a grid to represent the skin on the skeleton. The movement of bones drives the movement of the skin. There is a hierarchical relationship between bones. The movement of a parent joint affects the movement of children joints. The vertices on the skin grid have a set of weights corresponding to the bones. The weights determine how much a bone affects skin vertices. When the bone moves, the affected vertices on the skin should be recalculated according to the bone transformation matrix. For each skin vertices, all the weights from the joints who affect the given skin vertices are summed with the product of the transformation matrix to get the position of the vertices after the movement.

The human skeleton motion uses forward kinematics to find the rotation matrix of each joint one by one from the root joint. To obtain the bone rotation matrix, we must get the axis of rotation and the angle of rotation of the bone. When the human skeleton moves from the original state to the destination state, we can determine the rotation axis and the rotation angle with the skeletal direction vector in the original state and the direction vector of the posture in the destination state, and find the rotation matrix by the Rodrigue formula.

The skinning algorithm is the core of skeletal animation [20, 21]. Each joint information is collected by Kinect, and the transformation matrix between the bones is calculated. In order to bind the bones and skin vertices, the transformation matrix of each bone in the 3D virtual human motion is calculated by the linear blending skinning algorithm. In this way, SimuMan converts the original recognized joint points into the final skeleton motions, and realizes the 3D virtual human motion effect.

3.2 Personalized Facial Expression

This section describes facial expression from three perspectives of appearance, posture, and emotion. The appearance depicts the appearance of a person's face, such as fat or thin, big eyes or small eyes; the posture depicts the pose of a face, such as looking up, bowing, opening mouth,, and blinking. The emotion depicts a variety of facial expressions,, such as happiness, anger, sadness, and so on. SimuMan generates various 3D virtual faces with these three parts. Figure 2 presents the framework for generating personalized facial expressions.

SimuMan can capture 68 key points in a face image [22]. According to the key features of a standard face model with a neutral expression, SimuMan deforms the original standard face mesh model using the Radial Basis Function for a personalized 3D mesh model. After that, SimuMan attaches face texture on the mesh model to obtain a 3D virtual face.

SimuMan tracks face postures in the video sequence and calculates the position of the 68 face feature points in real-time. Using the improved pose estimation algorithm, SimuMan transforms 2D face images to their 3D models in real-time, meanwhile obtains

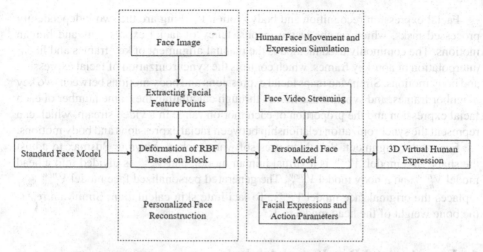

Fig. 2. The framework for generating personalized facial expressions

corresponding rotation and translation matrices. Through the calculated rotation translation matrices, the 3D virtual face moves in real-time while the 2D face image moves in the video stream.

SimuMan recognizes facial expressions according to face images in the video stream. Then it uses Facial Animation Parameters (FAP) to generate face animation based on the principle of MPEG-4 face animation, which uses three parameters to define facial expressions and animation. Facial Definition Parameters (FDP) describes the appearance model and texture of a face; FAP describes the basic facial expressions; Facial Animation Parameter Unit (FAPU) is the basic unit that represents facial animation parameters. For each input FAP value, SimuMan first finds the influenced area by FAP and the motion factor of each vertex in the area, and then calculates the target position of each mesh vertex in the area through the motion factor. After calculating the target position of each vertex, the mesh deformation can achieve facial expression animation.

In the synthesis of facial expressions, SimuMan calculates the weight of the input FAP value, the new target position of a face model, and deforms the mesh in order to realize the synthesized emotion expression of a virtual human. Finally, SimuMan can continuously represent facial expressions from one to another by setting parameters.

3.3 Synchronization of Human Motions and Emotions

To synchronize human motions and emotions, SimuMan aligns facial expressions and body motions temporally and spatially. Frame alignment solves the inconsistency between facial expressions and body motions at different times. Model alignment can unify body motions and facial expressions in the same measured scale even though they are made separately from different spaces. After the alignment, SimuMan realizes the personalized facial expressions of a virtual human according to the face personalized deformation algorithm and facial expression generation algorithm.

Facial expression recognition and body motion tracking are the two independently processed tasks, which results in the inconsistency of facial expressions and human motions. The commonly used method is the manual alignment of key frames and linear interpolation of non-key frames, which controls the synchronization of facial expression and body motions. SimuMan maps facial expressions and body motions between two key neighbor frames, and synchronize frames through calculating the frame number of each facial expression and the proportion of each motion range in a video stream, which can represent the synchronization relationship between facial expressions and body motions.

For model alignment, SimuMan uses software such as Maya or 3dsmax to adjust the shape of a model. V_t^{new} is a virtual human model, and V_t^{new} is divided into a head model V_{head}^{new} and a body model V_{body}^{new}. The generated personalized face model $V_{new\_head}^{new}$ replaces the original face model V_{head}^{new}. To facilitate skin calculation, SimuMan resets the bone weight of the head model to 1.

4   Experimental Results and Analysis

4.1   Experimental Results

SimuMan implements the presentation of virtual human limb motions in multiple scenes, and captures real human motions to show various gestures of a virtual human, such as raising hands, stretching hands, kicking legs, jumping, squatting down, lifting the leg, and so on.

Figure 3 presents three images for each group, which are virtual human, skeleton, color map detected by Kinect from left to right. Here are four sets of actions, which are standard action in the upper left, lifting a leg in the upper right, stretching a hand in the bottom left, raising hands in the bottom right.

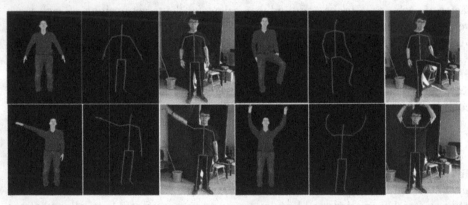

Fig. 3. Different body motions

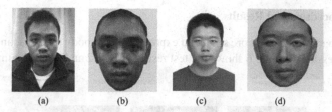

(a)   (b)   (c)   (d)

Fig. 4. Generated personalized 3D face models. (a) and (c) are the two different frontal faces, and (b) and (d) are the corresponding personalized faces

SimuMan can generate personalized 3D face models. Figure 4 presents the generated 3D face models for two different person.

SimuMan is an enhanced virtual human prototype system, enabling the modeling of facial expressions and their simulations of virtual humans, and supporting six kinds of facial expressions of sadness, surprised, happiness, anger, enjoyed, and neutral, as shown in Fig. 5.

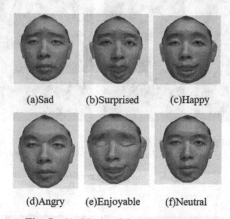

(a)Sad   (b)Surprised   (c)Happy

(d)Angry   (e)Enjoyable   (f)Neutral

Fig. 5. Six kinds of facial expressions

Meanwhile, SimuMan realizes the simulation of limb motions of virtual humans. Figure 6 shows body motions made by people daily, which are 'swing left hand', 'swing right hand', 'lifting left leg', 'lifting right leg', 'squatting down', and 'stretching hands'.

In addition, SimuMan realizes a real-time synchronization of facial expressions and body motions, and can maintain a continuous facial expression changes, which makes virtual human more vivid. As shown in Fig. 7, the left picture shows that the avatar waves happily to others, and the right picture shows that the avatar spreads its hands when it is sad. In the experiment, we use two cameras in the entire scene, one for observing human motions, and the other for close-up facial expressions.

Figure 8 presents the synthesized facial expressions. The left presents 75% surprise and 25% sadness. The right presents 50% happiness and 50% surprise. This synthesis of partial expressions enriches facial expressions by virtual humans in different scenes.

4.2 Test Procedure and Results

We invite 20 participants to score six facial expressions, ten body motions, and synthesis of facial expressions. Figure 6 shows the test results. Table 2 and Table 3 summarize the test results.

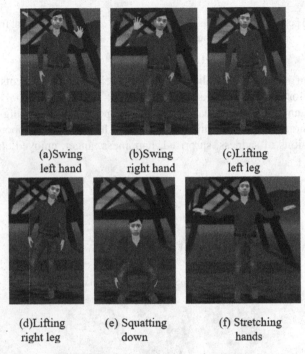

(a)Swing   (b)Swing   (c)Lifting
left hand   right hand   left leg

(d)Lifting   (e) Squatting   (f) Stretching
right leg   down   hands

Fig. 6. Daily body motions

Fig. 7. Synchronization of body motions and facial expressions of a virtual human

As we can see that the average MOS of the six emotions supported by SimuMan is 3.61; the average MOS of the ten motions is 4.12; the average MOS of the mixed emotions is 3.6. The results demonstrate that SimuMan meets the requirement of a public usage and achieves a good user experience.

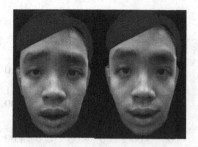

Fig. 8. Expression fusion

4.3 Test Plan

We invite 20 normal participants to test the SimuMan system. We adopt the mainstream mean opinion score (MOS). After the preliminary training, each participant has a certain understanding on shape distortion and presence delay in the SimuMan system. We use the method of subjective quality evaluation without the reference to let each participant test in an independent and quiet environment. Then we invite each participant to score the facial expressions and body motions generated by SimuMan. Table 1 presents the scoring benchmark.

Table 1. The MOS subjective scoring benchmark

Level	MOS score	User satisfaction
Excellent	5.0	Very good, no distortion and delay between the virtual model and real one
Good	4.0	Less delay, slightly distorted
Medium	3.0	Normal, some distortion, some delay
Poor	2.0	The motion recognition is not accurate, and the distortion is serious
Inferior	1.0	Extremely poor, completely distorted, with a huge delay

Table 2. The score results (participant 1–10#)

Score		1#	2#	3#	4#	5#	6#	7#	8#	9#	10#
Emotion	Enjoyable	3.20	3.30	3.00	3.30	3.00	3.50	3.50	3.50	3.00	3.00
	Happy	3.00	3.00	3.20	3.10	4.00	4.00	4.50	4.00	4.00	4.00
	Surprised	3.50	3.10	3.90	4.00	5.00	4.00	3.50	3.00	3.50	3.00
	Natural	4.00	5.00	5.00	5.00	3.00	5.00	4.00	3.30	4.00	4.00
	Angry	3.30	4.10	4.10	4.20	4.00	3.30	3.50	3.00	3.30	3.00
	Sad	4.00	3.20	4.00	4.00	4.00	4.00	3.00	2.00	3.00	4.00
	Ave.MOS	3.50	3.62	3.87	3.93	3.83	3.97	3.67	3.13	3.47	3.50

(*continued*)

Table 2. (*continued*)

Score		1#	2#	3#	4#	5#	6#	7#	8#	9#	10#
Motion	Raising hands	5.00	5.00	5.00	5.00	4.00	4.10	4.00	4.00	3.00	4.00
	Stretching hands	5.00	5.00	5.00	5.00	4.00	4.00	4.50	4.00	5.00	4.00
	Kicking right leg	5.00	5.00	5.00	4.00	4.00	4.00	4.00	4.00	4.00	4.00
	Kicking left leg	5.00	5.00	5.00	5.00	4.00	4.20	4.00	4.00	3.80	4.00
	Jumping	5.00	5.00	5.00	4.00	3.00	4.00	3.50	4.00	4.00	4.00
	Swing right hand	5.00	5.00	5.00	5.00	4.00	4.00	4.50	4.00	5.00	5.00
	Swing left hand	5.00	5.00	5.00	5.00	4.00	4.00	4.50	4.00	5.00	4.00
	Lifting left leg	5.00	5.00	5.00	5.00	4.00	5.00	4.00	4.00	3.90	4.00
	Lifting right leg	5.00	5.00	5.00	5.00	4.00	5.00	4.00	4.00	4.00	5.00
	Squatting down	5.00	5.00	5.00	5.00	4.00	5.00	4.50	4.00	3.00	3.00
	Ave.MOS	5.00	5.00	5.00	4.80	3.90	4.33	4.15	4.00	4.07	4.10
Mixed emotion	Happy-surprised	3.20	3.90	4.00	4.00	3.00	4.00	4.00	3.50	3.20	3.00
	Surprised - sad	4.00	4.00	4.00	4.00	4.00	3.00	4.00	3.50	4.00	4.00
	Sad - enjoyable	3.50	3.50	3.50	3.00	5.00	4.00	4.00	3.50	3.50	3.00
	Enjoyable - angry	3.10	3.10	3.50	4.00	2.00	3.00	4.00	4.00	4.00	3.00
	Ave.MOS	3.45	3.63	3.75	3.75	3.50	3.50	4.00	3.63	3.68	3.25

Table 3. The score of each tester (tester 11–20)

Score		11#	12#	13#	14#	15#	16#	17#	18#	19#	20#	Ave. MOS
Emotion	Enjoyable	3.90	3.00	3.00	3.00	3.00	3.00	3.10	3.00	3.00	3.00	3.17
	Happy	3.80	4.00	4.00	4.00	4.00	4.00	4.00	3.00	4.00	4.00	3.78
	Surprised	3.10	3.20	3.00	4.00	3.00	3.00	4.10	3.00	2.90	4.00	3.49

(*continued*)

Table 3. (*continued*)

Score		11#	12#	13#	14#	15#	16#	17#	18#	19#	20#	Ave. MOS
	Natural	4.00	4.00	4.00	4.00	3.00	4.00	4.00	4.00	4.00	4.00	4.07
	Angry	3.50	3.20	3.50	3.00	3.00	3.00	3.00	4.00	3.30	3.00	3.42
	Sad	4.00	5.00	4.00	4.00	4.00	4.00	4.00	3.00	4.10	4.00	3.77
	Ave. MOS	3.72	3.73	3.58	3.67	3.33	3.50	3.70	3.33	3.55	3.67	3.61
Motion	Raising hands	3.90	4.00	3.00	4.00	4.00	4.00	4.00	4.00	3.90	4.00	4.10
	Stretching hands	4.00	4.00	3.00	4.00	4.00	4.00	4.00	4.00	3.80	4.00	4.22
	Kicking right leg	4.00	4.00	3.00	3.00	3.00	3.00	4.20	4.00	3.00	4.00	3.91
	Kicking left leg	4.00	4.00	4.00	3.00	3.00	4.00	4.00	3.00	3.00	4.00	4.00
	Jumping	4.00	4.00	3.00	4.00	4.00	3.00	3.50	3.00	3.10	4.00	3.86
	Swing right hand	5.00	5.00	4.00	4.00	4.00	4.00	4.00	4.00	3.00	4.00	4.38
	Swing left hand	5.00	5.00	3.00	4.00	4.00	4.00	4.00	4.00	3.00	4.00	4.28
	Lifting left leg	5.00	4.00	3.00	4.00	4.00	4.00	2.90	4.00	4.10	4.00	4.20
	Lifting right leg	5.00	4.00	3.00	4.00	4.00	4.00	2.80	4.00	4.00	3.00	4.19
	Squatting down	4.00	5.00	3.00	4.00	4.00	4.00	3.10	4.00	4.00	3.00	4.08
	Ave. MOS	4.39	4.30	3.20	3.80	3.80	3.80	3.65	3.80	3.49	3.80	4.12
Mixed emotion	Happy-surprised	3.00	3.30	3.10	4.00	4.00	4.00	4.10	4.00	4.00	4.00	3.67
	Surprised - sad	4.00	4.20	4.00	4.00	4.00	3.00	4.00	3.00	3.00	3.00	3.74
	Sad - enjoyable	3.20	3.10	3.00	4.00	3.00	4.00	3.00	4.00	3.10	4.00	3.55
	Enjoyable - angry	4.00	3.40	3.10	4.00	4.00	4.00	3.20	3.00	4.00	3.00	3.47
	Ave.MOS	3.55	3.50	3.30	4.00	3.75	3.75	3.58	3.50	3.53	3.50	3.60

5   Conclusion

Metaverse is the next generation gaming Internet, in which a vivid virtual human plays an important role for a satisfied user experience. There are many challenges in achieving the real-time and simultaneous simulation of facial expressions and body motions of a virtual human. Unlike other studies which usually focus on the representation of either face expressions or body motions, this paper presents SimuMan, a simultaneous real-time method for representing motions and emotions of virtual humans in metaverse. With the experimental evaluations, SimuMan shows its practical performances of low presence latency, good robustness, good interactivity, and simplicity to use. And it can not only generate personalized virtual humans, but also can synchronize body motions and facial expressions of a virtual human. In addition, the blending of emotions enriches facial expressions of virtual humans. However, there is still a gap for mirroring a real-time and simultaneous representation of body motions and facial expressions made by a real human. In future, we will continue to improve the system performance in presence delay and 3D model quality.

Acknowledgement. This work is supported by NSFC project (Grant No. 62072150).

References

1. Kamal, S., Jalal, A.: A hybrid feature extraction approach for human detection, tracking and activity recognition using depth sensors. Arab. J. Sci. Eng. **41**(3), 1043–1051 (2016)
2. Poppe, R.: A survey on vision-based human action recognition. Image Vis. Comput. **28**(6), 976–990 (2010)
3. Thomasset, V., Caron, S., Weistroffer, V.: Lower body control of a semi-autonomous avatar in virtual reality: balance and locomotion of a 3D bipedal model. In: 25th ACM Symposium on Virtual Reality Software and Technology, 4, pp. 1–11 (2019)
4. Tong, X.L., Xu, P., Yan, X.: Research on skeleton animation motion data based on Kinect. In: ISCID 2012 Proceedings of the 2012 Fifth International Symposium on Computational Intelligence and Design, vol. 2, pp. 347–350 (2012)
5. Wang, C.C.: Adaptive 3D virtual human modeling and animation system in VR scene. Zhejiang University (2018)
6. Fang, X.Y., Yang, J.K., Rao, J., et al.: Single RGB-D fitting: total human modeling with an RGB-D shot. In: ACM Symposium on Virtual Reality Software and Technology, vol. 24, pp. 1–11 (2019)
7. Dushyant, M., Srinath, S., Oleksandr, S., et al.: VNect: real-time 3D human pose estimation with a single RGB camera. ACM Trans. Graph. **36**(4), 1–14 (2017)
8. Pavlakos, G., Zhu, L.Y., Zhou, X.W., et al.: Learning to estimate 3d human pose and shape from a single color image. In: The IEEE Conference on Computer Vision and Pattern Recognition (CVPR), pp. 459–468 (2018)
9. Bogo, F., Kanazawa, A., Lassner, C., Gehler, P., Romero, J., Black, M.J.: Keep it SMPL: automatic estimation of 3d human pose and shape from a single image. In: Leibe, B., Matas, J., Sebe, N., Welling, M. (eds.) ECCV 2016. LNCS, vol. 9909, pp. 561–578. Springer, Cham (2016). https://doi.org/10.1007/978-3-319-46454-1_34
10. Huang, H., Chai, J., Tong, X., et al.: Leveraging motion capture and 3D scanning for high-fidelity facial performance acquisition. ACM Trans. Graph. **30**(4), 1–10 (2011)

11. Booth, J., Roussos, A., Ponniah, A., et al.: Large scale 3D morphable models. Int. J. Comput. Vis. **126**(2–4), 233–254 (2018)

12. Booth, J., Roussos, A., Zafeiriou, S., et al.: A 3D morphable model learnt from 10000 faces. In: Proceedings of the IEEE Conference on Computer Vision and Pattern Recognition, pp. 5543–5552 (2016)

13. Li, T.Y., Bolkart, T.J., Black M., et al.: Learning a model of facial shape and expression from 4D scans. ACM Trans. Graph. **36**(6), 1–17 (2017)

14. Feng, Y., Wu, F., Shao, X.H., et al.: Joint 3D face reconstruction and dense alignment with position map regression network. In: IEEE International Conference on Computer Vision, pp. 557–574 (2018:)

15. Wu, F.Z., Bao, L.C., Chen, Y.J., et al.: MVF-net: multi-view 3D face morphable model regression. In: Proceedings of the IEEE Conference on Computer Vision and Pattern Recognition, pp. 959–968 (2019)

16. Pavlakos, G., Choutas, V., Ghorbani, N., et al.: Expressive body capture: 3D hands, face, and body from a single image. In: Proceedings of the IEEE Conference on Computer Vision and Pattern Recognition, pp. 10975–10985 (2019)

17. Roth, D., Bente, G., Kullmann, P., et al.: Technologies for social augmentations in user-embodied virtual reality. In: ACM Symposium on Virtual Reality Software and Technology, pp. 1–12 (2019)

18. Patel, N., Zaveri, M.: 3D Facial model reconstruction, expressions synthesis and animation using single frontal face image. SIViP **7**(5), 889–897 (2013)

19. Tóth, A., Kunkli, R.: An approximative and semi-automated method to create MPEG-4 compliant human face models. Acta Cybern. **23**(4), 1055–1069 (2018)

20. Kavan, L., Sloan, P., Carol, S.: Fast and efficient skinning of animated meshes. Comput. Graph. Forum **29**(2), 327–336 (2010)

21. Sujar, A., Casafranca, J.J., Serrurier, A., et al.: Real-time animation of human characters' anatomy. Comput. Graph. **74**, 268–277 (2018)

22. Kazemi, V., Sullivan, J.: One millisecond face alignment with an ensemble of regression trees. In: Proceedings of the IEEE Conference on Computer Vision and Pattern Recognition, pp. 1867–1874 (2014)

Electric Transformer Oil Leakage Visual Detection as Service Based on LSTM and Genetic Algorithm

Mingliang Gao[1]([⊠]), Cihang Zhang[1]([⊠]), Chongyao Xu[1], Qi Gao[1], Jiwei Gao[1], Jing Yan[1], Weidong Liu[1], Xiaohu Fan[2,3]([⊠]), and Hao Tu[3]

[1] State Grid Beijing Changping Electric Company, Changping District, Beijing 102200, China
9420@whxy.edu.cn, zhangcihang0128@163.com
[2] Department of Information Engineering, Wuhan Collage, Wuhan 430212, China
[3] Jiangsu Titan Intelligence Technologies Co., Ltd., Wuxi 214000, China
htu@titan-os.com

Abstract. Power safety production has always been an important issue related to the national economy and people's livelihood in the energy system. For a long time, humans have relied only on manual inspection to monitor the transformer oil leakage hidden danger, through the camera multi angle continuous collection of data, and then used the long-term memory network and improved genetic algorithm combination, to solve the traditional statistical machine learning because the training sample is not enough to form artificial intelligence algorithm model of cold start problem. In this study, we used the architecture of cloud-edge collaboration to provide services. The complex large data model training is executed in the cloud, and then the model is written to the edge server for reasoning. At present, the system has completed the pilot operation in Beijing substation, and the operation effect is good. It can effectively identify all kinds of common oil leakage within 200 ms.

Keywords: LSTM · Genetic algorithm · Cloud-edge collaboration

1 Introduction

With the development of society, the demand for energy is increasing day by day. In the construction process, there is increase in all kinds of equipment, involving all production links. Safe production and facility protection are the core work related to the sustainable and healthy development of the industry [1]. The characteristics of energy production and the serious consequences of accidents will directly lead to serious political and economic consequences [2]. Safe and stable operation is of great significance [3]. The general office of the State Council, the national energy administration and other relevant government departments have issued documents for many times, taking safe development as the general policy and strategy to guide safe production [4], emphasizing that safety should always be put first, and highlighting the basic role of safety in development. These documents strengthen the red line awareness and bottom line thinking, effectively

© Springer Nature Switzerland AG 2022
B. Tekinerdogan et al. (Eds.): ICIOT 2021, LNCS 12993, pp. 90–101, 2022.
https://doi.org/10.1007/978-3-030-96068-1_7

safeguarding the safety of people's lives and property, and promoting the sustainable and healthy development of the industry.

Scholars in the field of electric power have shown great interest in artificial intelligence technology since its development. Traditional artificial intelligence methods, such as expert system, artificial neural network, fuzzy set theory and heuristic search, have been widely used in power system for a long time, which are mainly reflected in the fields of energy supply, power system security and control, operation and maintenance and fault diagnosis [5], power demand and so on. There are five areas in the power market. Based on the new generation of artificial intelligence, the combination of high-definition audio and video technology and AI technology can effectively improve the identification details [6], support the abnormal detection function of transformer oil leakage, effectively improve the safety guarantee ability [7], and provide the whole process safety protection for safety production.

2 Related Works

The monitoring of transformer oil leakage has not been properly solved for a long time. Many studies have put forward different solutions. such as, thermal detection [8], Infrared thermography (IRT) applications [9], and unmanned aerial vehicles [10] automatic cruise watch collects video information [11], combines 3D reconstruction and digital twin to realize autonomy [12]. There are also a lot of Internet of things devices [13], terminal devices to achieve the automatic duty of cloud side cooperation [14], through a variety of image information collection leakage problem [15].

However, the manifestations, causes and treatment methods of transformer oil leakage in power system include the following.

2.1 Manifestation of Transformer Leakage

Air Leakage.   Air leakage is an invisible leakage, such as the leakage of air in and out of casing head, diaphragm of oil conservator, glass of safety air passage and weld sand hole. Moisture and oxygen in the air will slowly penetrate into the transformer through the leakage parts, causing insulation damp and oil accelerated aging and other problems.

Oil Leakage.   Oil leakage is divided into internal and external leakages. Internal leakage refers to the leakage of oil in bushing or on load tap changer room to transformer body; external leakage refers to weld leakage and seal leakage, which is the most common leakage phenomenon. The typical oil leakage of transformer is shown in Fig. 1.

2.2 Causes of Transformer Oil Leakage

Manufacturing Quality.   In the manufacturing process of transformer, due to many welding points, long welding seam, difficult welding, welding material, welding specification, process and technology, the welding quality will be affected, resulting in air hole, sand hole, false welding and desoldering, which will lead to oil leakage of transformer.

Fig. 1. Oil leakage at the top and bottom of transformer

Failure of Sealant. Leakage of transformer often occurs at the joint, and more than 95% of it is mainly caused by sealant. The quality of sealant mainly depends on its oil resistance. If the oil resistance is poor, the aging speed will be faster, especially at high temperature. It is very easy for seal aging, cracking, deterioration, deformation and even failure to occur resulting in oil leakage of transformer.

Improper Installation of Gasket. When the gasket is installed, its compression is insufficient or too large. When the amount of compression is insufficient, and when the operating temperature of the transformer increases, the heated volume of the oil increases, resulting in oil leakage of the transformer, with large amount of compression, serious deformation of the gasket, accelerated aging and shortened service life.

Improper Flange Installation Method. Due to the uneven flange connection, the force around the gasket cannot be evenly applied during installation, resulting in non-uniform force on the bolts around the gasket. In addition, the flange joint deformation dislocation, is such that the gasket on one side of the force is too large, on one side of the force is too small, on the other side of the force is too small, the gasket on the small side is easy to cause leakage due to insufficient compression.

2.3 Treatment Methods

At present, most of the oil leakage detection methods are based on experience, and there is no accurate instrument for detection, which is the same in the power industry. Taking the oil leakage detection of oil immersed transformer as an example, the common practice adopted by power supply companies is: when the equipment operation and maintenance personnel make regular inspection, they use a white flashlight to illuminate the oil leakage points of oil immersed transformer such as bushing, butterfly valve, gas relay connection and the ground below them, and distinguish them by 'visual inspection' and 'nose smell'. From the long-term experience of substation inspection, it was found that the efficiency of using traditional methods to find transformer oil leakage is often greatly affected by work experience. When using traditional methods to find transformer oil leakage, it takes a lot of time and has low efficiency, which is not conducive to the daily inspection work of substation to be completed on time, according to quantity and quality. Although the fluorescence detection technology based on the fluorescence characteristics of transformer oil can shorten the time for inspectors to find the leakage point of transformer, relatively improve the work efficiency of inspectors, and make up for the lack of experience of some new employees to a certain extent, the fluorescence effect can hardly be observed by naked eyes in outdoor sunshine. Therefore, this method is only applicable to the transformer installed indoors or must be inspected at night, so its application has certain limitations.

The traditional way relies on manual regular inspection, which has low efficiency and time blind area. AI services can work continuously without rest.

3 Solution Architecture

3.1 Hardware Deployment

In order to verify the effectiveness of the transformer oil leakage anomaly detection algorithm based on human brain like continuous learning in real environment, the substation and other places with necessary data acquisition and artificial intelligence model reasoning equipment were selected. The demonstration application is developed around the algorithm model to show the detection effect of abnormal oil leakage of transformer in an intuitive way. It can be divided into the following parts: data acquisition subsystem: through the research on the leakage mechanism and historical data of transformer oil leakage, qualitative and quantitative analysis of the influence of different factors on transformer leakage from different aspects, as well as various specific appearances caused by it. Therefore, on this basis, design and deployment of the basic data acquisition system include the selection of test site and transformer equipment, the type of data acquisition, the type of acquisition equipment used, the installation location of equipment, the data transmission mode, etc. It realizes the unified data acquisition, storage and analysis, which is convenient for the subsequent algorithm design, training and evaluation (Fig. 2).

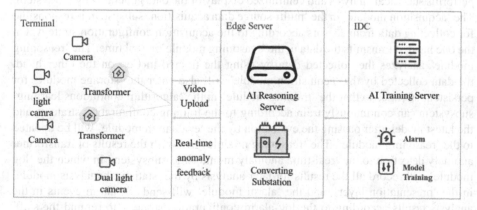

Fig. 2. Abstract architecture of deployment

After calculation, each edge computing node equipped with NVIDIA Tesla T4 GPU graphics card can process 18 channels of camera data. The number of edge nodes is determined by the number of cameras in each substation. Generally, each transformer needs 6 cameras. In this way, the monitoring environment for oil leakage in cloud edge collaborative computing is completed.

3.2 Software Architecture

The overall architecture of the system is shown in Fig. 3. The core layer completes the core function process of multi-source data acquisition model efficient reasoning and algorithm continuous learning real-time exception monitoring.

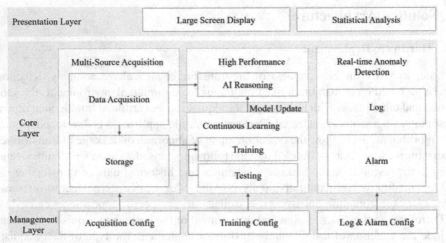

Fig. 3. Software architecture of oil leakage surveillance system

The management layer provides different management configurations, which can configure the acquisition, training, reasoning and monitoring modules. The display layer performs statistical analysis and centralized display of the data generated by the system. The 'acquisition module' in the 'multi-source data acquisition' subsystem is responsible for collecting data from sensors according to the acquisition configuration strategy. On the one hand, it transmits the data to the 'reasoning module' in real time. The 'reasoning module' analyzes the collected data by using the trained model; on the other hand, the data collected by the 'acquisition module' will also enter the 'storage module' for persistent storage, so that the 'training module' in the 'algorithm continuous learning' subsystem can continuously train according to the training configuration strategy, and the latest model after passing the evaluation by the 'evaluation module' will be updated to the 'reasoning module'. The 'reasoning module' will push the results of transformer anomaly detection to the 'real-time anomaly monitoring' subsystem, in which the 'log module' will record all the results for later analysis by the 'statistical analysis module' in the 'presentation layer', and the 'alarm module' will send out alarm events in the analysis results according to the log alarm configuration strategy to remind the staff.

Important statistical results and alarms will be visually displayed in the 'large screen display module' to conveniently display the effect of abnormal oil leakage detection of transformer.

Thus a typical cloud edge collaborative environment is completed, the intensive model training work is completed by IDC center node, and the model reasoning calculation is handed over to the edge node.

3.3 Functional Modules

This project mainly studies fore aspects.

Data Acquisition and Analysis Methods. The basic data acquisition system is designed and deployed, including the selection of test site and transformer equipment, the type of data acquisition, the type of acquisition equipment used, the installation location of equipment, the data transmission mode, etc., in order to realize the unified data acquisition, storage and analysis, and facilitate the subsequent algorithm design, training and evaluation.

Brain-Like Learning. Based on human brain like learning, this paper studies the algorithm framework and network structure of human brain like learning, and designs and improves the algorithm for practical problems and data. Combined with the actual needs of equipment inspection, the evaluation methods and indicators are studied and determined. Through repeated model training and evaluation on a large number of normal data sets, the evaluation results and algorithm implementation complexity, computational complexity and model size are comprehensively evaluated, and the algorithm framework and network are determined. According to the actual deployment requirements, combined with artificial intelligence reasoning hardware, the algorithm performance is further optimized.

Dynamic Online Learning. Based on the continuous training method of dynamic model online learning, the method of continuous data acquisition, training and verification suitable for transformer oil leakage anomaly detection is studied. With the gradual verification method, new data is continuously injected into the training data over time, and the model version is continuously updated, in order to make corresponding adjustments to the model according to the changes. The abnormal oil leakage detection is realized to adapt to the changes of different environments.

Pilot Deployment. In order to verify the effectiveness of the transformer oil leakage anomaly detection algorithm based on human brain like continuous learning in the real environment, the pilot deployment of transformer oil leakage anomaly detection is carried out by selecting qualified substations and other places, supplementing the necessary data acquisition, artificial intelligence model reasoning and other equipment. The demonstration application is developed around the algorithm model to show the detection effect of abnormal oil leakage of transformer in an intuitive way.

4 Oil Leakage Detection

Due to the rapid development of deep learning in recent years, the conventional image recognition algorithm and network architecture have been perfect enough, and the accuracy of recognizing people and objects can meet the requirements. Here we will not repeat the conventional identification, but only explain the core idea of transformer oil leakage. First of all, the probability of oil leakage is very small, so the training samples are very few. We adopt the LSTM model to continuously learn the "normal" state through the camera, and then form the long-term memory contour. When the newly acquired image deviates from the contour threshold, it can effectively capture the sudden large-scale jet, leakage and other dangerous scenes.

The AI detection algorithm for oil leakage is divided into two parts. Firstly, the video data source is obtained, in which the normal state is used as the training set, and the LSTM algorithm is used to calculate the safe contour. When the contour threshold is exceeded, it may be abnormal and need to be judged manually, which inherits the excellent characteristics of deep learning. Sparse contour can identify unknown security risks and solve the problem of insufficient training data. However, the samples of oil leakage scene anomaly are small, we use genetic algorithm for routine detection, and improve the genetic algorithm by floating-point coding, in order to speed up the convergence speed, simplify the operation difficulty, and shorten the training time. The anomaly recognition based on genetic algorithm can effectively reduce the amount of training data, and can maintain a high accuracy. Finally, the two models are summarized and used synthetically (Fig. 4).

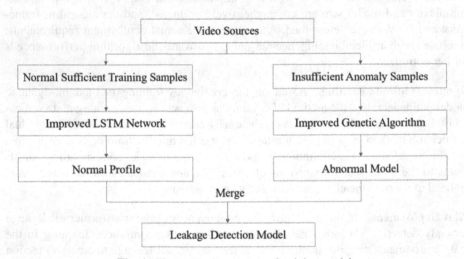

Fig. 4. The generative process of training model

Long term and short-term memory network algorithm has long been the classic algorithm of time series. It has the ability to extract the long-term pattern of the sequence, so that the normal situation can be memorized as a contour. The extended causal convolution network can be used for reference in the model, and the network architecture is shown in Fig. 5.

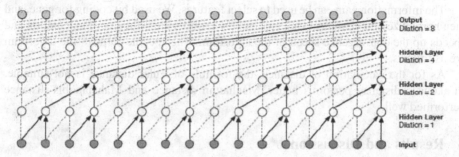

Fig. 5. Dilated causal convolutional network [16]

Because there are not many oil leakage events, the amount of sample data collected is not enough to support the training of traditional AI algorithm, so we employed genetic algorithm, which is a classical search algorithm inspired by biological evolution and natural selection, and has a wide range of applications. We used this genetic algorithm, starting from the sample image called the primary population, to segment the image features, to encode the samples at bit level, and then to generate a new next generation by means of crossover and mutation. Finally, we used the fitness function to calculate the fitness of each sample, and select the sample with the highest fitness as the new parent, and a gup of samples can be obtained by iteration. In the application of this project, we only extracted the features of the oil leakage area through image processing, and filtered out the part of the normal transformer. Then the feature selection algorithm based on information gain was used to select the optimal feature subset to reduce the computational complexity. We used information entropy to measure the purity of sample set. Assuming that the proportion of k-class samples in the current sample set D is p_K (k = 1,2,..., | y |), then the definition formula of information entropy of sample set D is as follows (1):

$$\text{Ent(D)} = -\sum\nolimits_{k=1}^{|y|} p_k log_2 p_k \tag{1}$$

Generally speaking, the larger the $Ent(D)$, the higher the purity of the partition by using attribute a. Suppose that the discrete attribute a has V possible values {a^1, a^2,···a^v}, If a is used to divide the sample set D, V branch nodes will be generated. Among them, the V branch node contains all the samples in D whose value is a^v on attribute a, marked as D^v. First, we calculate the information entropy of D^v according to formula (1). Considering the different number of samples contained in different branch nodes, we give the weight $|D^v|/|D|$, that is to say, the more the number of samples, the greater the influence of the branch nodes. Therefore, we use formula (2) to calculate the information gain obtained by dividing the sample data set D.

$$Gain(D, a) = Ent(D) - \sum_{v=1}^{v} \frac{|D^v|}{|D|} Ent(D^v) \tag{2}$$

The information gain can be used to select features. We used bit coding for gene, and then normalized the features, which effectively reduces the difficulty of calculation and speeds up the convergence speed of the algorithm. The specific steps of the algorithm are as follows:

As for the calculation of distance, the formula of Euler distance is not suitable. Minkowski distance performs better, Manhattan distance and Mahalanobis distance performed well.

5 Results and Discussion

After the completion of the system development, pilot application was carried out in Machikou substation of Changping District, Beijing. Through six star-light level 1080p cameras and 156 preset positions, a 110 kV transformer can be monitored from all-weather and multi angle. The deployment position of the camera is shown in the red dot in Fig. 6 and the required hardware parameters are shown in Table 2.

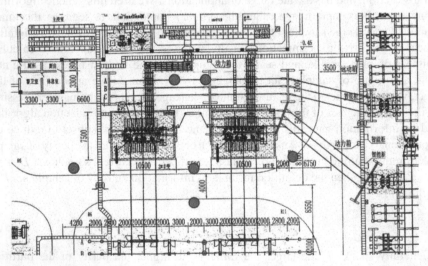

Fig. 6. Plan view of camera deployment around transformer

The interface of the application system is shown in Fig. 7, which is the Chinese version. The main functional modules include event management and site inspection, each probe is polling each key preset bit. During the trial operation, there was no transformer leakage accident. In fact, the probability of an accident is relatively small, about one in several million.

Table 1. Generation steps of anomaly detector

Generation steps of anomaly detector based on genetic algorithm

---

Input: Sample space *s*, maximum genetic algebra *n*, crossover rate *c*, mutation rate *p*, population number *m*.

Output: A sample of pictures representing the oil leakage $a_1,a_2,...,a_m$

for i in {1,2,...,n}do

  for j in {1,2,...,m}do

    Randomly select two from the sample space s as *Adam* and *Eve*

    Using cross rate *c* and cross operation to generate *child*

    Perform mutation operation on child using mutation rate *p*

    Distance between *child* and *Adam* is d_1, distance between *child* and *Eve* is d_2

    Calculate the fitness of the *child f*, fitness（x）=a/A

    Calculate the fitness of *Adam* is f_1, fitness of *Eve* is f_2

    if ($d_1<d_2$) and ($f>f_1$)

      Replace *child* with *Adam*;

    else

      if ($d_2<=d_1$) and ($f>f_2$)

        Replace *child* with *Eve*;

      end if

    end if

    a_j=child;

  end for

end for

Table 2. Required hardware configuration.

Equipment type	Configuration parameter	Quantity
CPU	Intel Core i7 6c12t @3.0 GHz	1
GPU	Nvidia Tesla T4	1
Memory	64 GB	32 GB * 2
Hard disk	240 GB Ent. SSD	1
	2 TB HDD	1
Network	Gigabit Ethernet	
Camera resolution	1920 * 1080	6

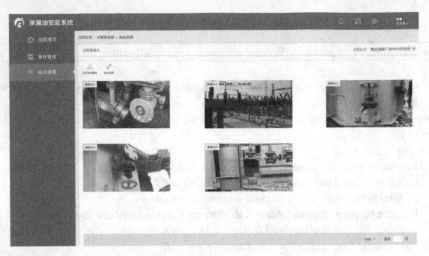

Fig. 7. Screenshot of application system interface

In order to test and evaluate the effectiveness of the system, the angle of the camera was adjusted and oil stains were applied on the same type of 110 kV transformer equipment, which has been insured, to simulate the occurrence of an accident. Then during the polling process of 156 preset bits, 20 preset bits prompt the alarm information and perfectly capture each position that is thought to be smeared with oil stains. The response time is about 200 ms, the capture parameter is 6 frames per second, and the rest is the time cost of network and computing reasoning. The comparison of the detected oil leakage is shown in Fig. 8, and the detected abnormal area is marked with a red box.

Fig. 8. Comparison of the detected oil leakage

References

1. Miller, B., Rowe, D.: A survey SCADA of and critical infrastructure incidents. In: Proceedings of the 1st Annual Conference on Research in Information Technology (RIIT 2012), pp. 51–56. Association for Computing Machinery, New York (2012)
2. Zhu, Q.Z., et al.: Development status and trend of global oil and gas pipelines. Oil Gas Storage Transp. **4**, 375–380 (2017)
3. Busogi, M., Shin, D., Ryu, H., Oh, Y.G., Kim, N.: Weighted affordance-based agent modeling and simulation in emergency evacuation. Saf. Sci. **96**, 209–227 (2017). https://doi.org/10.1016/j.ssci.2017.04.005
4. Tang, M., Mao, X., Tan, X. Zhou, H.: Engineering modeling unconventional emergency artificial society. Syst. Eng. Procedia **2**, 23–32 (2011)
5. Jumadi, Carver, S., Quincey, D.: A conceptual framework of volcanic evacuation simulation of Merapi using agentbased model and GIS. Procedia Soc. Behav. Sci. **227**, 402–409 (2016)
6. Shafiee, M.E., Berglund, E.Z.: Agent-based modeling and evolutionary computation for disseminating public advisories about hazardous material emergencies. Comput. Environ. Urban Syst. **57**, 12–25 (2016)
7. Danielski, I., Fröling, M.: Diagnosis of BuildingsâĂŹ thermal performance-a quantitative method using thermography under non-steady state heat flow. Energy Procedia **83**(2015), 320–329 (2015)
8. Fox, M., Coley, D., Goodhew, S., De Wilde, P.: Thermography methodologies for detecting energy related building defects. Renew. Sustain. Energy Rev. **40**(2014), 296–310 (2014)
9. Kylili, A., Fokaides, P.A., Christou, P., Kalogirou, S.A.: Infrared thermography (IRT) applications for building diagnostics: a review. Appl. Energy **134**(2014), 531–549 (2014)
10. Mauriello, M.L., Froehlich, J.E.: Towards automated thermal profiling of buildings at scale using unmanned aerial vehicles and 3Dreconstruction. In: Proceedings of the 2014 ACM International Joint Conference on Pervasive and Ubiquitous Computing: Adjunct Publication, pp. 119–122. ACM (2014)
11. Mavromatidis, L.E., Dauvergne, J.L., Saleri, R., Batsale, J.C.: First experiments for the diagnosis and thermophysical sampling using impulse IR thermography from Unmanned Aerial Vehicle (UAV). In: Qirt Conference (2014)
12. Rakha, T., Liberty, A., Gorodetsky, A., Kakillioglu, B., Velipasalar, S.: Heat mapping drones: an autonomous computer-VisionBased procedure for building envelope inspection using unmanned aerial systems (UAS). Technol. Archit. Des. **2**(1), 30–44 (2018)
13. Rajalakshmi, A., Shahnasser, H.: Internet of Things using Node-Red and Alexa. In: 2017 17th International Symposium on Communications and Information Technologies (ISCIT), Cairns, QLD, pp. 1–4 (2017)
14. Sandeep, V., Gopal, K.L., Naveen, S., Amudhan, A., Kumar, L.S.: Globally accessible machine automation using Raspberry pi based on Internet of Things. In: 2015 International Conference on Advances in Computing, Communications and Informatics (ICACCI), Kochi, pp. 1144–1147 (2015)
15. Yang, L., Shi, M., Gao, S.: The method of the pipeline magnetic flux leakage detection image formation based on the artificial intelligence. In: Proceedings of the International Conference on Video and Image Processing (ICVIP 2017), pp. 20–24. Association for Computing Machinery, New York (2017)
16. Oord, A., Dieleman, S., Zen, H., et al.: Wavenet: a generative model for raw audio. arXiv preprint arXiv:1609.03499 (2016)

MRA: Metaverse Reference Architecture

Liang-Jie Zhang[✉]

Kingdee Research, Kingdee International Software Group Co. Ltd., Shenzhen, China
zhanglj@acm.org

Abstract. On the basis of introducing the metaverse and the digital economy and supporting the development trend of new technologies, the concept of service-to-service (S2S) ecosystem is defined. The metaverse is used to build a virtual digital world and link the physical world. This paper focuses on the connotation of the two words Meta and Verse of the metaverse, and proposes a management framework of metaverse resources (Non-fungible token, 3D space, experience, avatar, etc.) in scenarios that support interactions such as the management of work, life, transaction, and customers. Then the paper proposes a metaverse reference architecture (MRA) for systematically constructing metaverse solutions. Finally, this paper also looks forward to the future development trend of the metaverse.

Keywords: Metaverse · Service-to-service (S2S) · Physical world · Virtual world · Resource management · Metaverse reference architecture (MRA) · Digital economy · Non-fungible token (NFT)

1 Introduction

Year 2021 is the first year of the opening of the metaverse. More and more large companies are supporting the development of this technology and application behind it, making the term metaverse flourish. For example, Microsoft started to promote the work of the enterprise metaverse, and wanted to extend the various application scenarios of the enterprise to the space of the metaverse [1]. Facebook believes that the metaverse is the future Internet, and plans to extend the capabilities of social networks to the metaverse [2].

The digital economy is a very important development direction in the world. It promotes not only the development of the Internet economy, but more importantly, it continues to promote the development of the traditional economy. From a technical point of view, I summarized the five most popular technologies at present. They are ABCDE shown in Fig. 1. A stands for artificial intelligence (AI), B stands for Blockchain, C stands for Cloud computing, D stands for big Data, and E stands for Everything is connected. I further subdivided E. It includes the Internet of Things technology (IOT) that links things to things, social network technology that connects people to people, and the ability to connect to the 5G network for terrestrial wireless communication, and metaverse technology that links the physical world with the virtual world. I think the metaverse is a new outlet for the digital economy.

B. Tekinerdogan et al. (Eds.): ICIOT 2021, LNCS 12993, pp. 102–120, 2022.
https://doi.org/10.1007/978-3-030-96068-1_8

Actually every new technology has only the only goal, which is to generate value around the users in the middle, that is to say, whether it is artificial intelligence technology, blockchain technology, cloud computing technology, or big data. The only way for these technologies to demonstrate value is to create value for the middle users. These new technologies often create value for the end consumers through services. In other words, the end user can subscribe to various services brought by various new technologies. For example, artificial intelligence can bring text recognition service, image recognition service, and video analysis service. They are all services one by one.

Every person, every organization, every software system, etc. in the world must show the ability to serve others. So the future world will be composed of services one by one. One of the best delivery methods for services currently is to use cloud computing infrastructure to deliver these services. The future world will enter a service-to-service (S2S) ecosystem. It turns out that B2B, B2C, B2B2C, etc. are actually not comprehensive. The future world is a combination of services to meet the needs of customer scenarios and provide solutions for them. These ABCDE technologies are used to create a new economic model, which is the digital economy.

Like other technologies, metaverse technology also needs to provide valuable services around the end user.

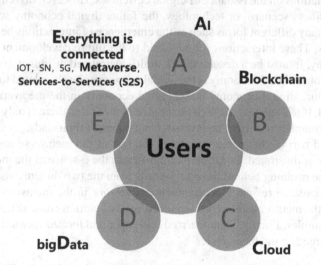

Fig. 1. A framework of new technologies and value realizations

The term digital economy appeared very early. In 1995, a book called "Digital Economy" [3] was published in the United States. At that time, the main supporting infrastructure of the digital economy was web pages or on the web server, all services are accessed online. At that time, online office and online approval applications appeared. Many business and transaction methods have moved towards e-commerce. Therefore, the two types of companies such as eBay and Amazon were created in that era. I call it *Digital Economy 1.0.*

An article in Forbes magazine in 2015 mentioned that the digital economy is an economic model created by digital technology [4]. This concept is still very easy to understand. I think the ongoing digital economy should belong to the era of *Digital Economy 2.0*. Its infrastructure is cloud computing, and various business applications are fragmented and service-oriented to provide users with value. In the current trading transactions, 70% to 80% are from mobile terminals, so now it belongs to the era of mobile e-commerce. The cloud computing era emphasizes resource sharing. The current digital economy model is mainly based on resource sharing to generate value. All resources can be shared in a service-based way and value can be generated in a service-oriented way.

With the continuous emergence of various new technologies, the development of the digital economy will enter the 3.0 era. The infrastructure supporting *Digital Economy 3.0* will be blockchain and metaverse. You have seen the constantly emerging digital application scenarios in the metaverse, plus the ever-enriching digital application scenarios in the physical world. Our various businesses will gradually be decentralized or multi-centralized, and another important point is immersion. We must be immersed in a virtual society in 360° to interact with people and services. The transaction methods in the metaverse will also move towards digital currency. Sovereign countries will also have new regulations on the issuance of digital currencies. However, driven by the metaverse as a business scenario or technology, the future digital economy will definitely demonstrate many different forms such as the emergence of interactions between multiple metaverses. These interactions actually lead to the future development mode of our digital economy. It must be a decentralized, multi-centralized or immersive one.

The traditional digital economy is the digital economy closely related to the physical world. The future digital economy is the digital economy in the metaverse and in the physical world. If it is calculated based on the size of the space, there is only one physical world, but the number of virtual metaverses can be tens of thousands.

The second part of this paper introduces the rise of the metaverse and the way in which its value is illustrated. The third part introduces the essence of the metaverse, and understands the meaning behind these two words from the two dimensions of Meta and Verse, and proposes a resource management framework in the metaverse. The fourth part proposes the metaverse reference architecture as a solution construction framework with some examples. Finally, I summarized this paper and looked forward to the future development trend of the metaverse.

2 The Rise of the Metaverse

In March 2021, a company called Roblox [5] was listed in the United States. This company is actually a platform for children to create and use games. On this platform, many high school students create their own games and use various components on this platform to build games in various scenarios. When it went public, several high school students shared their returns on the stock market to show the value of this platform. This is also the first listed company to clearly indicate that it is a metaverse company and has attracted the attention of many investors. Its stock price has almost maintained a market value of around 40–50 billion. It can be seen from the company's IPO that the metaverse was mentioned for the first time in the prospectus, making the metaverse a concept sought after by investors.

The metaverse itself is a term that was created a long time ago. There is a novel called "Snow Crash" [6], which mentioned the concept of metaverse. There was a movie called "Ready Player One" [7]. The movie describes how you will survive in a digital world after 2045. Need to find the key to control this digital space, then this movie describes the various tribulations to get this key. It mainly shows that he needs to transcend the existing society to find his spiritual sustenance, which means that he may be tired of the current life and want to experience a better life or create a completely different life. He thought of such an oasis, this oasis is the metaverse.

I summarized the connotation of the metaverse with Fig. 2. Its core has two features. The first is that you can build a virtual digital world. In the virtual digital world, you can build any objects, services, desired processes, etc., and the interaction between them. This is the construction level of the virtual world and the core part of the metaverse. The second part is to establish a connection with the physical world. I think the current metaverse is nothing more than the core content of these two aspects. In the process of constructing these two core contents, the well-known Internet technologies, AR, VR, and MR technologies, which are technologies for augmented reality and virtual reality, can all be used. If you want to build a lot of metaverses and allow one person to move in multiple metaverses at the same time, there may be more artificial intelligence robots in the future, so that artificial intelligence technology will also be used in this kind of virtual reality. In the construction of the avatar image in the world, a person can appear in multiple metaverses at the same time.

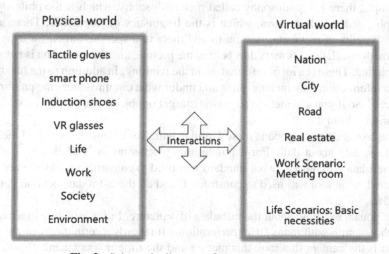

Fig. 2. Schematic diagram of metaverse interaction

We can show all the life and work in the physical world, as well as the concept of social environment and even the country, in the virtual digital world, and can also surpass. Then the link between the physical world and the virtual world is achieved through a series of technologies, such as tactile gloves, helmets, various induction shoes, various VR equipment, etc. They can all help establish a link with the virtual world. The link between the physical world and the virtual world can only be generated through interactive services in the end. For example, if the content of the PPT in the physical world is displayed on the screen in the virtual world, this is a link to a content presentation service. If I input the contents of the physical world keyboard into a device in the digital world, then this is the linkage of input services. The information in the virtual world can also be transferred to the physical world. So the essence of the metaverse is actually to establish a link between the physical world and the virtual world, and provide a series of methods, materials and tools in the virtual world to help you build the virtual world you want.

But no matter how you say it, from the perspective of English words, the metaverse is composed of meta and verse. Its prefix is meta, and the stem of the central word is verse. What kind of meaning do these two words represent? If you understand the meaning of the affix and the stem, it can really help you understand how the future metaverse should be constructed. Below I will explain what the metaverse means from its two core words, and which technologies can be used to build a virtual digital world and help link the physical world?

3   The Connotation of Meta and Verse

The first core word is the prefix meta. You can see from the dictionary that this word has many meanings [8], for example, it can be said to surpass existing objects and existing disciplines. This is one of its meanings. And there is a higher level of abstraction. For example, there is a philosophy called metaphilosophy, which is the philosophy of philosophy, and metalinguistics, which is the linguistics of linguistics. These are the example benefits of meta. If you want to add meta to a specific target, for example, a picture on the wall, there is meta data behind the picture, and the meta data is not visible on this picture. There is a lot of information in the painting. In addition to the handprints, the meta information may include when and under what circumstances the painting was constructed. So if you add meta to an existing target or object, you can see a lot of useful information behind it.

Some words that everyone is more familiar with, for example, are called metadata. Metadata is data about data. For example, many schemas in XML are all metadata. These metadata will tell you what standard was used to construct this data, when it was constructed, what tool was used to construct it, and all the extra data beyond your data is metadata.

Give you an example about the metadata of a picture. I took a picture in a museum. It is a phonograph with many 0101 perforations. It records a certain part of the music, but what is the camera that took this picture and the time it was taken? This is called metadata for images.

For software engineers, HTML is the language for constructing web pages on the Internet. One of the grammars in this language is meta, which must be followed by a name and corresponding content. For example, when someone visits this web page, the flowing code elements can automatically jump to a website like icws.org in 6 s. That is to say, information like meta is very useful. It can issue instructions to quote the original content. So everyone should see that the meaning of meta is far beyond its original content.

```
<meta charset = "utf-8">
<!-- Redirect page after 6 s -->
< meta http-equiv = "refresh" content = "6;url = http://www.icws.org">
```

There are a lot of applications in the meta field. It can be said that the Internet era in the past two to three decades is the era of meta. I remember when I was in 1996, we tried to extend the concept of hyperlink from text images to moving targets in the video [9], which means that when you watch a video over the Internet, there is a car moving in it with hyperlinks. You can also trigger the hyperlink on the car manually or automatically. At this time, the metadata is meta for video. So you can see that meta actually has a lot of meaning. With these technologies, you can build new methods of storytelling, movie construction, and even the current game play. The content of the script can be dynamically adjusted [10], this is the value brought by meta. In 1999, at MIT's Media Lab, Professor Janet Murray and her team used IBM's "HotVideo" technology to support meta for video to construct links and automatic switching of multiple completely different video scenes. Extending a person's role into the past and the future, and using this technology to re-tell how the future film industry and video industry will develop, so she took the name "eTV", which is enhanced TV [11].

As you can see, there are actually many scenarios you can imagine. The concept of meta is not only used in a streaming video over the Internet, but also in real-time live video or digital TV programs. When digital TV programs are on the air, you can insert a variety of information, including product information, at any desired time node and location [12]. It can be seen that meta has been accompanied by the development of the entire Internet. Various other content can be embedded in the live broadcast. This is the value that meta brings for live broadcasting. It helps us think about how to surpass existing goals and surpass existing resources to extend them to bring more value when constructing various digital worlds in the metaverse.

The second word is verse. There are some explanations of verse in the dictionary, but in the word Metaverse, a better annotation is the abbreviation of universe [17], which will help us construct the metaverse in the future. The universe is a combination of known or hypothetical objects and all phenomena in the entire space. This is actually the same as the "heaven, earth and everything in one body" mentioned in Chinese philosophy. It also talks about the universe including the whole world, especially about human beings. It is also mentioned that the universe is a world or domain in which something exists or prevails, which means that the universe can be industrial, territorial, and regional. Especially in the field of science and technology, there is such a definition of the universe. It refers to the combination of matter, energy and space. It also includes the content between the solar system, galaxies and galaxies, and the universe is still expanding. These insights are all can be used to help build the future metaverse.

When it comes to building a virtual universe, it's not that no one has done it, but many people have tried doing it. For example, a company born in California in 2003 is called Second Life [18]. It builds an online game creation and play platform. It is a game content provider. With the rise of the current concept of Metaverse, the platform behind it that supports online game construction has been stripped and sold. At present, this company is only left with the operation of games and the operation of metaverse services.

In the digital metaverse to be built, you can extend everything in the existing physical universe into the digital world, and you can also build the energy in the virtual world and other various services, and even beyond the imaginations in the current physical world.

4 Resource Management of Metaverse

In the world of the metaverse, it also manages resources. Based on the analysis of different metaverse scenarios, the resource management in the metaverse is nothing more than two elements: first, sort out what resources you have in the metaverse; second, around these resources, how to manage, how to create value. From the perspective of resources, you have avatar, space, immersive experience and content, and digital assets, such as NFT. How to value resources is a management issue. Management is divided into many scenarios. The concepts of country, world, company, work, life, etc., can all exist in the metaverse. Therefore, the digital management of enterprises will become more complicated in the metaverse.

As shown in Fig. 3, there are several types of resources in the metaverse. It includes a variety of platforms, contents, services and assets, which form the most important elements in the virtual metaverse. Components and services are presented in an immersive experience. For example, the ability to build a platform allows you to build a lot of three-dimensional spaces in the digital world, build the shapes you want, and create creative products and services.

From the management perspective, we want these resources to generate value in the metaverse, which is consistent with our management goals in the physical world. In addition to managing resources, we must also manage the corresponding finances. Therefore, financial management, supply chain management, human resource management, project management, etc. in the metaverse are all directions worth exploring. In terms of team management, it includes social communication and virtual studios. In order to build valuable services in the virtual space, you have to attract customers and stick to them. So you need to manage customers, and you must also do marketing and promotion in the virtual world.

If you have a scenario for building an online learning platform, you must first think about whether to rely on an existing metaverse platform or build a metaverse platform yourself. When choosing to rely on an existing platform, all you have to do is to build business scenarios, corresponding educational content, and related services on this platform. This needs to stand out in the creation of scenes and content.

In addition, to visit some web pages in the Internet age, you start with a search engine or URL. But in the future in the metaverse, although a website is also given on the experimental metaverse platform now, it may become another direct naming method in the future. For example, *University A* on a metaverse platform can also be cultivated into a very famous brand, and this brand can be accessed without a URL or link. I think there will be a new addressing technology similar to DNS in the metaverse. But no matter which industry or field you do, you must attract your users and continue to create value for users, so that you can remain attractive in the metaverse.

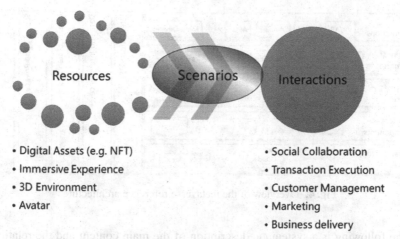

- Digital Assets (e.g. NFT)
- Immersive Experience
- 3D Environment
- Avatar

- Social Collaboration
- Transaction Execution
- Customer Management
- Marketing
- Business delivery

Fig. 3. Scenario-based resource interactions for the metaverse

As described in the application scenario of creating a university in the metaverse, the core of the metaverse is management and operation. The goal of management is to carry out resource management around various application scenarios in the metaverse. The following will introduce how to design an architectural model of the metaverse solution in a systematic way, and provide a reference architecture for the construction of metaverse solutions that adapt to various scenarios.

5 Metaverse Reference Architecture (MRA)

The essence of the metaverse is the 360-degree immersive Internet, and it is a symbiotic environment of the physical world and the virtual world. When building various application scenarios or platforms in the metaverse, many technologies are interlinked, and many ways of thinking are also corresponding to the Internet era. It's just that the original flat content displayed on the webpage is now extended to a 360-degree social environment that can be infinitely expanded. This paper extends the SOA reference architecture [13] and Cloud Computing Open Architecture [20] to metaverse, and proposes the basic framework of Metaverse Reference Architecture (MRA) as shown in Fig. 4, which helps to systematically show the creator's service design and operation ability. The services layer in the SOA reference architecture is extended to the services store layer in MRA. In the age of Service-to-Service (S2S), the architectural components in each layer can be offered as a service.

For different roles, the scenes and solutions for entering the metaverse can be diversified. For example, for content and scene builders, after buying assets in a certain metaverse, they need to ask service providers to help design business scenarios, to help you build the buildings you want, and to help you design the services you want to provide. In addition, the consumer is a service-using role that resides in the metaverse. Therefore, the metaverse contains three key roles, namely the builder of the platform, the builder of content and scene services, and the consumer of the service.

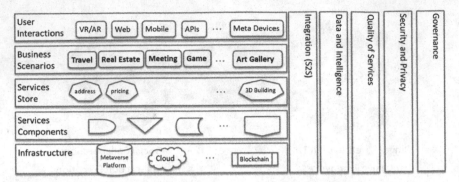

Fig. 4. Overview of the metaverse reference architecture

The following is a systematic description of the main content and the relationship between the layers of the MRA around the ten layers.

5.1 User Interactions

The user interaction layer is the channel for metaverse users to carry out various activities and interactive services corresponding to the business scenario. Representative channels can be VR, AR or MR apps, Internet web pages, mobile apps, program interface APIs, and other future emergence of the metaverse input/output applications.

The channels corresponding to the user interaction layer have various technical implementation methods. At present, there are many integrated system including software applications and supporting sensors to access the virtual digital world. The current sensor technology is very different from before. In addition to being small, it can also feel the weight of the object you pinch like a human hand. It is an immersive sensor and can also extend many abilities of the facial features. Including current VR glasses, AR equipment, MR equipment, as well as touch gloves, can feel the weight of water, etc., which are all technologies required by the physical world. The applications of embedding these hardware technologies can enable you to interact with services in the virtual world in real time.

These sensing technologies based apps or APIs have also laid a very good foundation for us to enter the metaverse era, and these interactive technical standards for entering the metaverse are also gradually being improved.

In terms of interactive application, Microsoft's Mesh [1] supports many VR headsets. These headsets allow us to interact with you through mixed reality, that is, there is a hologram in the physical world to interact with you. Mesh application can now also be used on computers, tablets, and even mobile phones.

In the exploration of Web 3.0 [17], protocol-extensible user interface cradle ("browser") is also one of the modes of user interaction.

5.2 Business Scenarios

The business scenario layer is the general term for various business solutions in the metaverse that can attract users and continue to create value for users in a specific field or industry. It has a relatively complete life cycle as a business offering.

Compared with the physical world, the business scenarios in the metaverse will also undergo a lot of changes. For example, the way *people communicate* with each other will change again. Especially when you are eating with your friends and family members, most of the time everyone is playing with their mobile phones, and they rarely communicate. They are either using WeChat, TikTok, or Facebook. The current way of communication has been changed once, no longer by writing or calling, but this change is only on the two-dimensional plane of a mobile phone, and it is ours to be changed again in the future. We will turn ourselves into an avatar or multiple avatars, placed in a completely different 360-degree immersive social environment. That is to say, we will go from the flat anti-social to the 360-degree social interaction in the future. When you are in the virtual immersive environment at 360 degrees, you will naturally want to interact with others. So our space will be equipped with devices. Maybe this device is not as big as it is now. It may be a very small device. You will be able to play in multiple virtual metaverses.

In addition, how to *sell our products in the virtual world*, which is the e-commerce in the physical world. When companies are doing digital transformation in the future, will they still use the Internet e-commerce platform that they have been using for 20 years? Metaverse can become another option, and it may surpass our traditional e-commerce model.

You can *build your own space with metaverse components* according to your ideas. Compared with writing code to develop applications, it will be a disruptive change.

Therefore, in the future, what many companies may need is for the metaverse to provide such business tools, and use these tools to help companies build business scenarios for the metaverse. For example, using the metaverse can share the resources of the airport, share the service capabilities and training capabilities of the airport, and then use the airport metaverse platform to help everyone buy and sell. Therefore, companies still have many opportunities to innovate on the channel of digital transformation. If the innovation speed is fast, every company must follow up with such a pace. This is just one of the business scenarios of how to work in the virtual world in the future. What should our workspace look like? How to extend the limited airport space to infinity? When 100 million people go to and from the airport a year, but we did not provide the opportunity to attract them to participate in the interaction, which requires us to provide valuable services.

There are many business scenarios in the metaverse, such as *collaborative creation*. Everyone can design a house and a product together in the metaverse space, and communicate around the physical shape and characteristics of the product. You can also outline the strategy for the next few years, just like the participants are on a public display board and work collaboratively. The immersive business scenario is the most important thing, because it will make you feel that participants are working together, as if someone is by your side, a human-like experience of the scene, it is a 360-degree full-scene virtual metaverse.

In addition, the scenes of food, clothing, housing and transportation in the metaverse will be very rich. For example, the experience of *traveling in the metaverse* will change. You can invite your friends or family members thousands of kilometers away to go to a metaverse space or a metaverse park to play together. You can *experience all kinds of things* such as exciting exercise, and you actually only need to stay at home to open a metaverse application and operate the corresponding device. You can also *visit an art marketplace*, see the artists and staff who are creating, and interact with them.

5.3 Services Store

The service store layer is a collection of reusable services used to build various business scenarios. Generally speaking, some services can be directly combined with each other, and a large part of services can be combined through the integration layer's technology to meet more and more complex business scenarios. Using cloud computing technology, various resources can be shared in the form of services. In theory, the architectural components in any layer of the metaverse reference architecture can be shared as a service and become a member of the services store layer. The service classification of the service store layer can be carried out according to the metaverse itself corresponding to the solution, which can be industry classification, field classification, or other refined classification and management as needed.

The following introduces several types of sample services that are more important in the construction and interaction of the metaverse.

Avatar Customization Service: A person in the physical world can be mapped into an avatar in the metaverse. You can use the avatar customization service to design your image, which can be designed into various avatars you want, which can be video, picture, or some of the avatar templates that come with it.

Modeling Service: In the virtual world, you not only have to build the model of the spatial concept of the house, but also model the various characters and objects inside. You can also model their movement, as well as the interaction between modeling objects.

Interactive Service: This kind of interaction must be like the experience of interaction between people, and its delay requirements are also very high. It just happens that the 5G connection delays up to about one millisecond. In the future, we hope that there will be higher-speed network technologies that can help the physical world and the virtual world to produce an interactive experience with almost zero delay.

Transaction Service: The core blockchain technology is included in the transaction service. Because in the virtual world, all assets will be digitized. The valuation and evaluation of digital assets, such as the introduction of NFT, etc. are just some of them. The core supporting technology is decentralized or multi-centralized blockchain technology, which can ensure the uniqueness of each digital asset.

Content Creation Platform Service: Use this platform to build various content or various business scenarios in the virtual world, and help merchants settled in this metaverse to generate value through the services provided by the merchants. For example, a metaverse platform suitable for a specific scene or a specific region can be used in the metaverse of real estate, the metaverse of aviation, and the metaverse of airports. A platform provides various components for you to assemble and create all kinds of content you want. In terms of content production services, such as Microsoft's Mesh application [1], it can help you configure the corresponding interactive equipment, and is equipped with creative tools to model and build the VR space. You can use these tools and some of its built-in components to design all kinds of immersive scenes that you can't imagine. The builder of the actual scenario is sometimes like the owner of a company. You have to build your business model, build your entire business scenario and the services you can provide. Then these services mainly rely on some content creation platform providers which provide you with a lot of tools. Adobe has launched a platform called Aero [19], which allows you to easily build a lot of virtual assets in the environment in contact with the physical world. For example, you can decorate a house in the virtual space, and you can extend the painting you are currently drawing to an extra space. The most important thing is that we can add a lot of dynamic sense to our traditional artworks, and use AR technology to build a virtual metaverse.

Corresponding to the *business scenario that extends the airport space to infinite*, it can be constructed by the following three example reusable services. The first service is the *space rental service* for participating in the metaverse conference. Many small spaces can be set up in the airport to equip them with high-end devices, and they can be used to participate in "face-to-face" meetings in the virtual world. It is to rent out the equipment and physical space of the airport as a service to enhance the participation experience of the metaverse conference. At the scene of a virtual meeting, you can also import Zoom, WeChat video or Facetime from the physical world. There are screens, conference tables and chairs in the virtual meeting room. The metaverse conference system can link the physical world with the virtual world. After linking up, you can achieve many such entities, which is equivalent to having a meeting with a person in a meeting place in person. An example of a virtual meeting system is Workrooms [2] released by Facebook. The second service is *digital artwork service*. Some of the passengers who lead to the airport metaverse must have artistic talents. They can build many photos of highlight moments and other types of artworks of their own, and then NFT these artworks. Then the airport metaverse constitutes a platform for digital artwork display and trading. The third service is *flight experience and training service*. The airport has a lot of aircraft resources. Usually people are more interested in the latest aircraft and want to visit. According to this demand, we can build a new service in the metaverse. Everyone is invited to visit in the metaverse and learn to fly high-end airplanes in the metaverse.

Therefore, in the metaverse, *our working methods and the construction of corresponding business models will undergo very big changes*. The metaverse platform needs to refine reusable services suitable for different industries, different fields, and different scenarios, in order to build a rich variety of services.

5.4 Service Components

The service component layer refers to a collection of codes that implement various services in the service store layer, such as Java, JavaScript, Python, C, C# and other code types. The current low-code development platforms corresponding to their respective programming languages help to improve the efficiency of code development.

The *land sale service component* of the land sale service is a set of decentralized software applications. This service component needs code to implement many specific operations. For example, Decentraland [14] constructs various functions of the real estate metaverse. This application component first needs to map addresses in the physical world with addresses in the virtual world. For example, the number of streets in New York City, the naming of streets, and the arrangement of house numbers in the metaverse can all be exactly the same as in the physical world. It allows you to construct for each house number of land. Different prices are given for different plots. Some are worth two thousand, some are worth three thousand, and some are worth five thousand. This service component has to implement the valuation standard. The simple rules depend on the reputation of the building built on that location in the physical world and the owner's reputation, whether the building is magnificent enough for pricing. For example, the headquarters building of a certain company may be worth fifty thousand dollars, and an ordinary small facade may be worth one thousand dollars, which also laid some gimmicks for the promotion of projects in the metaverse.

Another major type of service component in the metaverse is the *construction service component*, which provides a series of capabilities to implement construction services. In the metaverse, you can use the various architectural designs, tools and materials provided by the system to build a house on your own land. It can also provide you with tools for various construction services. For example, you can build your own house. In the future, this house may become a school. The school business will need a set of tools for enrollment services, lecture services, and training services. It will provide you with tools plus your creativity and customized development to help you achieve it. If you want to make it into a museum, the various digital assets displayed in it, the various tools purchased, and the interactive tools, these service components can be provided to you through yourself or a third-party service provider. So what is built in the metaverse is not only content, but also valuable services based on these content, so that you can stick to your existing users. Just like Internet traffic, as long as you can provide enough sticky services, in this metaverse, the content or services of your metaverse will be more popular. And more people will be attracted to visit you, and the value of your metaverse will be greater. This is also why the greater the openness of the metaverse, the more active the service component suppliers participating in the construction of various tools.

Decentraland has also built its own digital currency called MANA in its metaverse. The *digital currency service component* is the customized code for landing the MANA service. It needs to deposit all the plots in the metaverse on the blockchain. This is completed by connecting to the open Ethereum system. The digital currency MANA itself has to establish links with the digital currency exchange platforms. The decentralized application of *land purchases and sales* is also a service component to provide transaction support to investors or some companies engaged in real estate business.

In addition, in the exploration of Web 3.0 [17], protocol-extensible developer APIs & languages is also one of the modes of service component development.

5.5 Infrastructure

The infrastructure layer is composed by various supporting infrastructures in the entire metaverse solution, including public metaverse platforms, sensors, blockchain support platforms, value support platforms, databases, legacy systems, cloud computing infrastructure, etc.

The user interaction service that connects the physical world and the virtual world mentioned in the user interaction layer is largely realized by relying on the apps or APIs of *sensor systems*. Being a member of the infrastructure layer, the traditional sensors are only used to obtain data and perform operations required by instructions. Now it comes to *immersive sensing*, which contains more meaning. For example, we are far away in different cities, can we have dinner together, can we transfer the taste of real meat in the physical world to the virtual world, so that the participants who have dinner together in the metaverse can feel the meat and other dishes taste. These are gradually being realized, and now all kinds of flavors can also be produced using corresponding materials or other methods.

The *value support platform* is the infrastructure for value evaluation and asset digitization. Our way of judging value is also changing. Now we think of valuable things as things that are visible and tangible. For example, computers and mobile phones are things that are visible and tangible, so we think they are valuable. In the virtual world, there are still many valuable content, such as digital assets in the virtual world. Digital artwork is an example of this. Digital assets will become a very important way of showing value in the metaverse. The infrastructure that supports the valuation of assets in the metaverse, such as NFT (Non-fungible tokens), is an important way of presenting value. For example, I have 100 dollars in my hand now, and I want to exchange it for 10 ten-dollar banknotes. Then among these banknotes, they are equivalent, and they can be replaced. Even if one of them is not banknotes, you can still use 8 ten-dollar banknotes, and then you transfer 20 dollars to me through PayPal or two 10-dollar PayPal transactions, each of which is actually replaceable. But what is irreplaceable here? For example, you have a hand-painted digital artwork. If we digitize all the metadata behind it and store it on the blockchain, it means that this hand-painted painting has one unique certificate on the blockchain and only one owner. Now the owner can go to auction this painting anytime. For example, the current price is one thousand US dollars. But as other people learn more about this handmade painting, usually this painting should be worth more money. After being sold for two thousand, three thousand, five thousand, twenty thousand, thirty thousand dollars, etc., then the process of buying and selling this handmade painting is a process of increasing the value of the unique digital asset. NFT has now become a popular way of displaying a digital asset in the metaverse, and then the *NFT system* has also become a very important part of the infrastructure in the metaverse solutions. Financial institutions such as Visa, in order to help its customers understand what the metaverse means to their future, it also released a white paper for the metaverse [15] to guide its customers to understand the metaverse's new concepts.

It is worth noting that although many countries are opposed to encrypted digital currencies, at least they do not encourage transactions. It is necessary to find suitable opportunities and scenarios to enable encrypted digital currencies to be linked with legal currencies. The main challenge here is that governments must find the right balance between regulation and innovation.

In the exploration of Web 3.0 [17], it mentioned zero/low trust metaprotocols (polka-dot), peer-to-peer (p2p) internet overlay protocols, platform neutral language and other meta-protocols, point-to-point Internet protocols, platform neutral languages, etc. The other architectural building blocks in the infrastructure layer including the public meta-verse platform, blockchain support platform, database, legacy system, cloud computing infrastructure will not be discussed in detail in this paper.

5.6 Integration

The metaverse's solutions are all composed of cloud services deployed on one or multiple cloud computing platforms to achieve various business capabilities. According to the complexity of service compositions, the integration layer of the Metaverse Reference Architecture mainly includes SOA based integration, low code integration and zero code integration.

SOA based integration is mainly used to integrate cloud services from different service providers and traditional software application systems (including legacy systems). It includes the integration of business logic and data by exposing APIs of various application systems. The complexity of this type of integration is relatively high.

Low code integration is mainly to encapsulate more business capabilities in advance to form service components that can be reused. In the process of service integration, a drag-and-drop method is used to integrate various services through reusable service components. In this mode, the business logic orchestration of the service composition requires less code to complete the integration work. The complexity of this type of integration work is relatively light, and the requirements for the professional capabilities of the coding work are relatively low.

Zero code integration mainly uses some zero-code development platforms to prepare the connection relationship between various cloud services in advance. When business workers compose multiple related cloud services that they need, they don't need to write any code, but only need to design the business logic.

Generally speaking, behind these three types of integration technologies are the docking of business logic and data flow. To complete the integration of the metaverse solutions to the ever-increasing number of cloud services, it is not recommended to adopt the point-to-point integration mode of connecting one service to another service. The complexity of this integration mode is very high. It is recommended to establish a standard data model in your own specific field or industry. After adapting the data of other vendors' cloud services to your standard model, integrating service becomes relatively simple. Such standard data models can be specifically defined in the data and intelligence layer in MRA.

In addition, there will be many public metaverse platforms in the future, and you can also build multiple metaverses on each platform. Naturally, there will be a problem, that is, how to communicate, exchange, and even interact among these metaverses.

When Web services were introduced about 20 years ago, the interoperability was a big challenge to form consensus and standards. Looking forward to the arrival of the metaverse, we need to explore to build a cross-metaverse language that can be used to interact and operate with each other. One of the possible ways is to record and share data that needs to cross the metaverse through the blockchain. Because in every metaverse, if your assets leave evidence on a public blockchain, a certain connection may be established. This is a direction that is worth exploring.

In the exploration of Web 3.0 [17], data distribution protocols, transient data pub/sub messaging are mentioned, they are all subordinate to the data distribution, format conversion, transient data subscription and publishing mechanism of the integration layer of the metaverse solution.

5.7 Data and Intelligence

The data and intelligence layer of the metaverse solution is the general term for general data architecture, data service specifications, and common artificial intelligence technologies related to data processing across business scenarios and technical systems.

Data is an important asset that runs through various business scenarios. When assets are transferred between different organizations, different departments, and different applications, data must be value-added in different links. One of the important means of value-added is integration of the professional capabilities at each node, and then using artificial intelligence technology, unearth the business insights behind the data, and allow the data to form a continuous value-added process in the flow of data to form a data value chain.

Data architecture is a unified framework for data norms for each enterprise. It involves all aspects of business processes, technical systems, and application systems. It also has a close relationship with the industry and field in which the enterprise is located. Especially when the industry has its own standards, it must be followed. When the industry has not yet formed a standard, the governance of data standardization should also be carried out within the enterprise. Data architecture, business architecture, application architecture, and technology architecture together constitute an enterprise architecture. They support each other and evolve dynamically, which are important cornerstones for building agile organizations and enterprises.

5.8 Security and Privacy

The security and privacy layer of the metaverse solution covers the role permissions of the avatars in the metaverse, and the corresponding strategies and systems for privacy management of data generated using various services in the metaverse.

The security of the system includes the safe storage of data, the safe transmission of data, and the management of data access rights. In terms of user identity and rights management, it must be integrated with the access rights of system applications, so that the user's role can be accessed between different applications. The security and privacy management mechanism may dynamically change based on business scenarios to ensure data security and ensure that authorized users can access applications with corresponding permissions.

When building a global metaverse solution, system privacy protection is particularly important. When constructing business scenarios, it is necessary to fully understand the needs of data privacy protection, and areas that require anonymity or desensitization must be processed in advance. It is also possible to use new technologies such as federated learning to continuously train data analysis models across departments, companies, and even countries using their own managed data instead of sharing data, so as to improve their business insights.

As one of the ways of technical implementation, in the exploration of Web 3.0 [17], zero/low trust interaction protocols (Bitcoin, Ethereum, parachains) and Second Layer protocols pointed out how to use blockchain technology to achieve a decentralized model to address the problems of trust interaction, encrypted channel management and encrypted storage.

5.9 Quality of Services

The quality of services layer in the metaverse covers every quality aspect of the business scenarios and technical realizations of the metaverse solution. Among them, the user experience for avatars in the metaverse is very important, and the definition and management of the quality of services provided for each avatar becomes very necessary.

The first type of service quality is the quality system in the virtual world similar to the traditional Internet environment, and its corresponding service quality mainly includes service-level-agreement (SLA) and so on. This includes service availability, concurrency delay, and customer satisfaction.

The second category is the quality of service in which the virtual world is connected to the physical world. There are parameters such as interaction delay rate, stability, distortion rate, etc. For example, in an application scenario that is closely connected with the physical world to discuss new directions or remote training, use augmented reality to show how a person is standing in front of you and interacting with you, compared to a real person's distortion rate? When participants design a product, practice calligraphy, or band ensemble together, the accuracy of the position of the pen on the drawing in the virtual space, the straightness and thickness of the line, and the response speed of the pen are all concerned by the participants of the metaverse in terms of the quality of services. One of the factors that affect the quality of services is the speed and quality of data transmitted between the virtual digital world and the physical world.

5.10 Governance

The governance layer of the metaverse solution refers to the general term for the various elements of laws, regulations, standards, organizational structures, and capability requirements that need to be followed in the process of creating the metaverse solution.

The life in the real physical world is very different from the life in the metaverse, including the constraints of laws, regulations, and morals in real life, while people in the virtual world have many desires, including dark bad ones. There are some violent or unsuitable materials or services in the metaverse. These problems must be considered and solved when constructing a metaverse solution. This is also very important in the governance of the metaverse solution.

When any new technology emerges, there will be ethical, moral or legal issues. Here we first regard the metaverse as a new technology. When the metaverse emerges, our people in the physical world have a set of laws that can be formulated corresponding laws, regulations and norms in the metaverses. It looks just like we treat Internet technology. At the same time, in the virtual metaverse, when you construct the content of the services provided for others, you have to design your rules, usage guidelines and restricted usage scenarios. This is actually the process of designing your laws and regulations in the metaverse. If you are building scenes and content on an existing metaverse platform, then the metaverse platform you rely on should also have its own set of rules and governance systems.

When we really consume services in the metaverse, it will involve the superposition of a three-tier governance system. The first is the use of various norms for a specific metaverse in the physical world, and the second is the metaverse platform that restricts and regulates you. The third is that the content creator can set who can enter, which age group can enter, and which age group cannot enter in terms of scene or content level. When constructing, it is necessary to propose specific specifications and safeguard measures for the metaverse solution.

It is also necessary to establish a cross-organization metaverse COE (Center of Excellence) to promote the coordination and value combing of the entire solution's planning, design, development, launch, operation and promotion of the success of the entire solution.

6 Conclusions and Future Directions

Based on the introduction of the development of the metaverse and the service-to-service system, this paper believes that the two cores of the metaverse are the construction of a virtual digital world and a link to the physical world. Then the interaction of resources driven by scenes is used as the resource management framework of the metaverse. In order to build a metaverse solution on a large scale, the metaverse reference architecture (MRA) is proposed. MRA provides an architectural direction for the construction of a metaverse solution that adapts to various scenarios.

Based on the systematic thinking of the metaverse solution architecture introduced in this paper, the future development of the metaverse will continue to evolve and improve around the following four directions.

The first is *the immersive engineering of resources*, which means that our original resources should be placed in a socialized scene, and we should have an immersive feeling when interacting with others.

The second is *the digitization of interactions*. Real interactions can be achieved in the virtual world of the metaverse, just like humans operating resources in the physical world, there can be authentic and digitized interactions in the metaverse.

The third is *the servitization of scenarios*. If you want resources, interactions, or scenarios to generate value, you must turn them into services to export their capabilities. For example, if you build a house and turn it into a museum, then the museum exhibition service is an example of servitization. To build a school, it is necessary to create admissions services to obtain the corresponding return on investment.

The fourth is *the valuation of services*. In order to generate value for service capabilities, we need to find the end consumers who use these capabilities and services, and let the end users subscribe and consume the services in the various scenarios constructed in the metaverse.

As a matter of fact, the above four directions can be used as use cases while a metaverse solution is being designed and implemented.

References

1. Microsoft: Microsoft Mesh. Retrieved from Microsoft Mesh, December 2021. https://www.microsoft.com/en-us/mesh
2. Meta: Introducing Horizon Workrooms: Remote Collaboration Reimagined, 19 August 2021. https://about.fb.com/news/2021/08/introducing-horizon-workrooms-remote-collaboration-reimagined
3. Tapscott, D.: The Digital Economy: Promise and Peril in the Age of Networked Intelligence. McGraw-Hill, New York (1995)
4. Olenski, S.: 3 Steps to succeeding in today's digital economy, Forbes (2015). https://www.forbes.com/sites/steveolenski/2015/06/24/3-steps-to-succeeding-in-todays-digital-economy/?sh=7aee40f5872a
5. Roblox Corporation. Roblox. https://www.roblox.com/
6. Stephenson, N.: Snow Crash. Spectra (2003)
7. Spielberg, S.: (Director). Ready Player One [Motion Picture] (2018)
8. dictionary.com. meta. https://www.dictionary.com/browse/meta
9. Chen, J., Feig, E., Zhang, L.-J.: CN, US Patent No. US6175840B1(1996)
10. Bootcamp: Digital Entertainment. https://www.cbsnews.com/news/bootcamp-digital-entertainment/
11. Hot Norman eTV Prototype. http://penlab.gatech.edu/1998/01/17/hot-norman-etv-prototype/
12. Zhang, L.-J., Chung, J.-Y., Liu, L.-K., Lipscomb, J.S., Zhou, Q.: An integrated live interactive content insertion system for digital TV commerce. In: ISMSE 2002, pp. 286–295 (2002)
13. Arsanjani, A., Zhang, L.-J., Ellis, M., Allam, A., Channabasavaiah, K.: S3: a service-oriented reference architecture. IT Professional, pp. 10–17, May–June 2007. https://doi.org/10.1109/MITP.2007.53
14. Browning, J.H.: Are we in the Metaverse yet? New York Times (2021). https://www.nytimes.com/2021/07/10/style/metaverse-virtual-worlds.html
15. Castillo, N.B.: Visa enters Metaverse with first NFT purchase. Forbes (2021). https://www.forbes.com/sites/ninabambysheva/2021/08/23/visa-enters-metaverse-with-first-nft-purchase/?sh=747b063a68b3
16. https://www.dictionary.com/browse/universe
17. Web 3.0,https://web3.foundation/about/
18. Explore.Discover.Create. https://secondlife.com/
19. Augmented reality. Now a reality. https://www.adobe.com/products/aero.html
20. Zhang, L.-J., Zhou, Q.: CCOA: cloud computing open architecture. In: 2009 IEEE International Conference on Web Services, pp. 607–616 (2009), https://doi.org/10.1109/ICWS.2009.144

Author Index

Printed in the United States
by Baker & Taylor Publisher Services